To:
Peanut Butt —

Enjoy these beautiful
pictures

Love Auntie Carol
& Uncle Ron

12-25-05

HORSES

PUBLISHERS

TEXTS BY

GABRIELE BOISELLE

HENRY DALLAL

ATTILA KORBELY

PAOLO MANILI

SENIO SENSI

MEDFORD TAYLOR

**project manager
and editorial director**
VALERIA MANFERTO DE FABIANIS

graphic design
CLARA ZANOTTI

graphic layout
MARIA CUCCHI

editorial staff
GIADA FRANCIA
ENRICO LAVAGNO
ALBERTO BERTOLAZZI

translation
TIMOTHY STROUD

An imprint of White Star, Italy
© 2005 **WHITE STAR S.P.A.**
VIA CANDIDO SASSONE, 22-24
13100 VERCELLI - ITALY
WWW.WHITESTAR.IT

ISBN 88-540-0377-8

REPRINTS:
1 2 3 4 5 6 09 08 07 06 05

Printed in China
Color separation: Chiaroscuro, Turin

HORSES

1 ● Great Britain. The graceful profile of an Arabian.

2-3 ● France. The semi-wild horses of the Camargue.

4-5 ● USA. A herd of horses in the Southwest.

6-7 ● Italy. Pure competition at the Palio in Siena!

9 ● USA. This bay is distinguished by the white heart standing out on its forehead.

11 ● The Netherlands. Friesians boast proud and wavy manes

12-13 ● USA. An Appaloosa with a leopard coat.

14-15 ● Austria. A Haflinger pony galloping.

16-17 ● Argentina. A *gaucho* and Criollos on the pampa.

Introduction

by Paolo Manili

OVER THE MILLENNIA THE HORSE HAS EXERCISED AN IMMENSE INFLUENCE OVER THE DEVELOPMENT OF HUMANITY; CIVILIZATION WOULD HAVE EVOLVED DIFFERENTLY HAD THE CREATURE NOT EXISTED. IT WAS IN EARLIEST PREHISTORY THAT MAN TRANSFORMED THE HORSE FROM A TASTY PREY INTO A MEANS OF TRANSPORT, WORKING TOOL AND WAR MACHINE. IN ADDITION, BY AROUSING PASSIONS AND AMBITION IN MAN, THE HORSE GAVE RISE TO GREAT DEEDS, ENCOURAGED HUMAN MIGRATIONS AND CONQUESTS, AND DETERMINED HUMAN EVENTS AND DESTINIES. THE HORSE HAS ALSO INSPIRED COUNTLESS GENERATIONS OF PAINTERS AND SCULPTORS, POETS AND MUSICIANS, WHOSE REPRESENTATIONS OF THE HORSE'S

Iceland. A wavy mane frames the gentle gaze of an Iceland pony, a docile, affectionate and reliable animal.

Introduction

FORM, PERFORMANCE AND NATURE HAVE REFLECTED THE TENDENCIES OF EVERY CIVILIZATION AND CULTURE THROUGHOUT HISTORY. IN MYTHOLOGY, THE HORSE WAS FUSED WITH MAN TO FORM THE CENTAUR; IT WAS GIVEN WINGS TO BECOME A HIPPOGRIFF; IN REALITY, THE SPECIES ADAPTED TO EVERY CLIMATE AND ENVIRONMENT AND BECAME DEEPLY ROOTED IN HUMAN CUSTOMS AND BEHAVIOR. THE WAYS IN WHICH THE HORSE CONTINUES TO INFLUENCE OUR WAY OF LIVING, SPEAKING, DRESSING, THINKING AND DREAMING ARE NUMBERLESS AND BEAR WITNESS TO THE TIMES IN WHICH MAN AND HORSE COULD NOT DO WITHOUT EACH OTHER. WHERE MAN CONDITIONED THE NATURE OF HIS FOUR-LEGGED FRIEND BY CREATING DIFFERENT BREEDS, EACH SUITED TO A PARTI-

Introduction

CULAR PURPOSE (DRAUGHT, PACK, SADDLE AND RACE HORSES), THE HORSE CONTINUED TO INFLUENCE THE MODUS VIVENDI OF HIS MASTER-CUM-FRIEND. IN MORE RECENT TIMES, VEHICLES HAVE LARGELY REPLACED HORSES IN THEIR DAILY TASKS, YET, FOLLOWING A MASSIVE BUT BRIEF DECLINE IN THEIR PHYSICAL PRESENCE, THEY HAVE BEEN RETURNED TO FASHION THROUGH A GROWING ENVIRONMENTAL AND ANIMALIST AWARENESS THAT HAS RESULTED IN THEIR ESTABLISHING THEMSELVES AS POPULAR RECREATIONAL COMPANIONS. THUS THEY STILL RACE ON FAMOUS COURSES, COMPETE AT THE OLYMPICS, POPULATE FARMS AND THE COUNTRYSIDE, AND ALLOW TOURISTS AND OTHERS TO ENJOY THE BEAUTY OF NATURE FROM A SADDLE. THERE IS AN ENGLISH SAYING 'THERE ARE

Introduction

TWO TYPES OF PEOPLE: HORSE RIDERS AND NEUROTICS,' THUS SUMMING UP THE MODERN RELATIONSHIP BETWEEN MAN AND HIS MOUNT, ONE THAT GOES BEYOND PSYCHOLOGY. AND THIS RELATIONSHIP HAS BEEN TAKEN FURTHER TO INCLUDE RIDING THERAPY, IN WHICH THE HANDICAPPED BENEFIT FROM A RELATIONSHIP WITH A HORSE. THE SPLENDID PHOTOGRAPHS IN THIS BOOK ILLUSTRATE THE THREE THOUSAND YEARS OF THE HORSE WORLD ON PLANET EARTH. IT IS A WELL-MERITED TRIBUTE TO OUR COMPANION – WHO HAS WORKED FOR US, FOUGHT FOR US AND PATIENTLY TRANSPORTED US.

23 ● France. A powerful and very arched neck gives the Arabian horse a very noble appearance.

24-25 ● Great Britain. A cavalry regiment on parade in one of London's streets.

26-27 ● Austria. A Lipizzaner from Vienna's Spanish Riding School performs perfect acrobatics.

28-29 ● Barbados. A Thoroughbred is first across the line in a this race.

BREEDS

and their

CHARACTERISTICS

GABRIELE BOISELLE

• France. A splendid Arabian sorrel.

INTRODUCTION Breeds and their Characteristics

Some breeds just tug at one's heart, but above all others the Arabians do. Charming, beautiful, intelligent and playful, they are eager to connect with people; they are curious about everything new and try to please their humans, whom they believe to be their own. Then there are Friesian horses, absolutely gentle and humble with those who work with them day by day. But the moment they are free, they fly over the earth, no longer earthbound, with their floating manes and 'feathers' around their legs and their huge tails which seem to be created of waves of black hair. They

Portugal. A white Lusitanian plays in Mediterranean waves.

WERE BRED TO IMPRESS IN FRONT OF THE SPECIAL FRIESIAN SJEEß WITH THEIR EXTENDED TROT. BUT WHILE THEY ARE GREAT DRESSAGE HORSES THEY ARE ALSO IDEAL FOR CIRCUS WORK. NO HORSE SHOW CAN EXPECT TO SUCCEED WITHOUT THE PERFORMANCE OF FRIESIAN HORSES. THEIR CLOSE RELATIVES, THE ANDALUSIANS, WHICH ARE MOSTLY GREY HORSES WITH FLOATING MANES, CAN BE ADMIRED AS WELL IN THE DIFFERENT DISCIPLINE OF HIGH-STYLE DRESSAGE. CENTURIES AGO THEY WERE BRED TO PERFORM THE CAPRIOLE AND PESADE AS USEFUL FIGHTING STRATE-GIES IN BATTLE. LATER ON, HORSEMANSHIP BECAME AN ART AND TODAY THE LIPIZZANER HORSES PERFORM THESE FIGURES IN THE SPANISH RIDING SCHOOL IN VIEN-

INTRODUCTION Breeds and their Characteristics

NA. ALL OVER EUROPE THERE ARE DIFFERENT BREEDS OF HORSES DESCENDED FROM FOREBEARS BRED FOR SPECIAL MILITARY NEEDS: CAVALRY HORSES FOR WAR; HORSES EASY TO RIDE; AND FAST HORSES ABLE TO JUMP OVER OBSTACLE. THEN THERE ARE THE WORKING HORSES; HEAVY BREEDS FOR PULLING WAGONS, TRANSPORTING GOODS, AND FOR PLOWING FIELDS. ON SUCH HORSES' SHOULDERS LAYING THE RESPONSIBILITY FOR AGRICULTURAL LIFE. IN THEIR MILLIONS THEY BROUGHT IN THE HARVEST AND ASSURED WEALTH AND PROSPERITY. SADLY, WITH THE ADOPTION OF INDUSTRIAL MACHINERY MOST OF THEM WERE NO LONGER NEEDED AND WERE SLAUGHTERED. ONLY A DECADE AGO DID PEOPLE BEGIN TO UNDERSTAND

THAT THEY HAD TO PRESERVE THESE OLD BREEDS IN RECOGNITION OF ALL THE WORK THEIR ANCESTORS HAD DONE. AS A RESULT, THERE IS NOW A RENAISSANCE IN THE BREEDING OF DRAFT HORSES IN EUROPE AND AMERICA. OLD BREEDS LIKE THE ARDENNER, PERCHERON, NORIKER, BRETONE, COB NORMAND, SHIREHORSE, CLYDESDALES AND OTHERS ARE BECOMING KNOWN AGAIN, HORSE LOVERS VERY OFTEN UNDERESTIMATE THE VALUE OF PONY BREEDS. THEY ARE SEEN AS KIDS' HORSES, NOT TO BE TAKEN SERIOUSLY. BUT NOW, WHEN THE PRICE OF A 'SPORT' PONY CAN EASILY BE TRIPLE THE PRICE OF A REASONABLY ACCOMPLISHED SHOW HORSE, PEOPLE ARE HAVE BECOME AWARE OF THE POTENTIAL VALUE OF

INTRODUCTION Breeds and their Characteristics

THE "SMALL ONES." IN FACT, OVER HISTORY, PONIES HAVE BEEN USED IN AGRICULTURAL WORK AND IN PULLING WAGONS, JUST LIKE DRAUGHT HORSES. FOR EXAMPLE, IN NORWAY, THE FJORD PONY FROM WAS USED ON THE VERY STEEP HILLS ALONG THE FJORDS, WHERE BIGGER HORSES HAD TOO LITTLE ROOM TO WORK SUCCESSFULLY. IN IRELAND, THE CONNEMARA PONY WAS ONCE A REAL WORKING BREED THAT PULLED CARTS. ONLY ON THE WEEKENDS DID THE FARMERS RACE THEM AGAINST EACH OTHER. TODAY THE CONNEMARAS PRODUCE SUPERCLASS JUMPING PONIES FOR INTERNATIONAL COMPETITIONS. FOR CEN-TURIES EVERY COUNTRY BRED THE HORSES IT NEED-ED. THE BLOODLINES OF MOST BREEDS HAVE BEEN IM-

Breeds and their Characteristics

Introduction

PROVED BY ENGLISH THOROUGHBREDS AND BY ARABIANS. BUT THE ACTUAL DIVERSITY OF THE BREEDS RESULTS FROM THE SELECTIVE BREEDING DIFFERENT BREEDERS HAVE UNDERTAKEN. IN THE FUTURE, WE WILL HAVE DEMANDS FOR HIGH-QUALITY STOCK, AND HIGH-INTENSITY DEMANDS AND PEOPLE WILL ALSO BREED THE HORSE MOST SUITABLE FOR COMPETITION AND FOR RECREATIONAL RIDING, EITHER BASED ON THE WESTERN OR ON THE ENGLISH RIDING SYSTEM. AND FINALLY, THERE IS ONE VERY IMPORTANT REASON TO BREED HORSES, NOW THAT WE NO LONGER NEED THEM TO ENSURE OUR DAILY SURVIVAL – THE LOVE WE FEEL FOR THEM IN GETTING TO KNOW THEM.

• Iceland. Rustic and tough, the Iceland has a thick mane.

The Netherlands. Detail
of a Friesian's raven-
black, finely curled mane.

42 • The Netherlands. The Friesian's legs are not very long and the hocks are rather hairy.

43 • The Netherlands. A black Friesian plays in the rain.

• The Netherlands. With their "curly" manes, Friesian horses boast unique elegance.

The Netherlands.
Friesian at the gallop in the
Dutch countryside.

48 • The Netherlands. Docile and intelligent, Andalusians are excellent dressage horses.

49 • The Netherlands. A bridled Andalusian during a horse show.

Portugal. The docile and brave Lusitano is a very rare horse. It is estimated that there are only 20,000 or so around the world.

Germany. The coats of Arabian horses vary in color, often with white splotches on the legs and head.

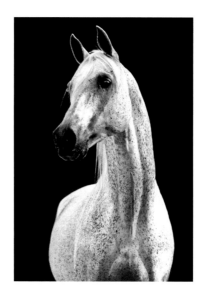

54 ● Germany. Excellent riding horses, Arabians are quite frisky.

55 ● Germany. A fine Arabian thoroughbred seems to pose proudly for the camera.

56 • USA. Among Arabian horses, black ones with white hocks are the rarest and most sought after.

57 • USA. Arabians are slender in build and of a nervous disposition.

58-59 • Spain. Traditionally used for riding, Arabians seem born to gallop.

60 and 61 • France. The sturdy head of a Comtois reveals its docile but willing nature.

62-63 • France. The Comtois, a French draught horse, in the Middle Ages they were used as warhorses.

Iceland. The Iceland pony can ridden, but it can serve as a packhorse or draft animal. Moreover, it does not need to be stabled during the winter.

66 ● Iceland. With its intelligent
eye and fringed mane, Iceland
ponies win sympathy at first glance.

66-67 ● Iceland. The Iceland
breed was created at the start of
the 20th century by crossing local
ponies with ponies that
Norwegians brought to the islands.

● Iceland. Seen here at the gallop in the snow, the Iceland is used as a saddle pony for inexpert riders.

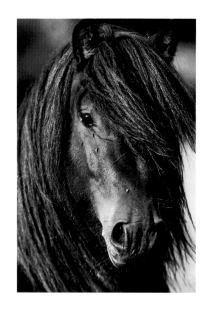

Great Britain. A long-established English breed from the Devon moors, the Dartmoor is strong and tireless.

Great Bretain. Though sturdy and unflagging, the long blond manes of Shetland ponies make them seem cuddly.

Great Britain. Shetland ponies, originally from the Scottish mainland, in particular from the Orkneys and Isle of Shetland, were originally used as draught animals in mines and agriculture.

76-77 ● Argentina. This close-up of a Criollo shows its tenacious and willing spirit.

77 and 78-79 ● Argentina. A saddle horse, the Criollo was derived from crossing Arabian, Berber and Andalusian horses brought to South America by the Spanish.

80-81 ● Argentina. The Criollo is the horse used by the *gauchos* of Latin America: they are sturdy, quick and agile in working with cattle.

82-83 ● Argentina. A Criollo's coat may be any of several shades, but is often marked with white and "mule lines."

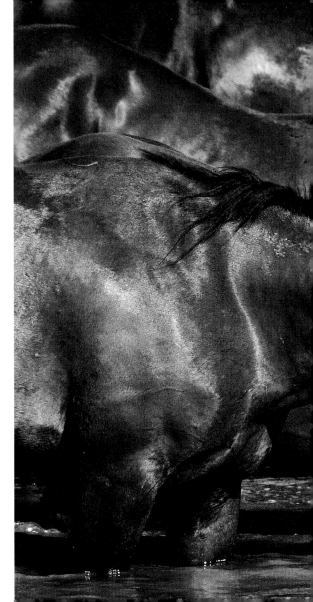

84-85 ● Italy. Balanced and strong, and a good jumper, the Maremmano is generally bay.

86-87 ● Italy. Originally short, strong and skittish, through crosses with English breeds the Maremmano has become the elegant and classic military horse of today.

Ireland. The Gypsy Vanner is not really a breed but a horse of changeable appearance.

• Ireland. A saddle horse used by the military, and originally from Ireland, the Gipsy Vanner is currently used in equestrian tourism.

Ireland. The Gipsy Vanner is tough and dynamic: here we see their elegance, thick mane, long tail and hairy hocks.

Ireland. Bred with black, bay, gray and sorrel coats, Gipsy Vanners are also attractive piebald.

96-97 ● Austria. The Haflinger is originally from the Tyrol and therefore is strong and tough, fully suited to the alpine environment.

98-99 ● Austria. The Haflinger is considered a pony by experts due to its short, sturdy legs.

100 and 101 ● Austria. This tyrolean pony's gentle expression belies a good and intelligent nature.

102-103 ● Austria. With their hooves hidden in the fresh snow, this Haflingers seems perfectly at home on the mountain slopes.

104-105 and 105 ● Austria. A herd of Haflingers rises to a gallop on a snowy meadow in the Tyrol.

106-107 ● USA. The Pinto was first bred by Native Americans looking for "colored" wild horses to cross with horses of Spanish origin.

108 ● USA. Gracefulness of gait, particularly at the gallop, is the Arabian's most appreciated characteristic.

109 ● USA. This Arabian foal shows all the lightness and elegance typical of the breed.

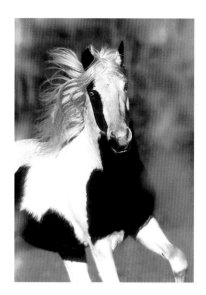

USA. The Comanches were the first to begin selection of the Pinto, and ended up with the piebald we know.

“ A LINEAGE AS NUMEROUS AND NOBLE AS THAT OF THE HORSE NATURALLY BOASTS GREAT "FAMILIES." THESE FAMILIES, COMMONLY KNOWN AS BREEDS, HAVE BEEN SHAPED BY MAN THROUGH THOUSANDS OF YEARS OF PATIENT WORK, AND HAVE CREATED THE MOST FORMIDABLE ALLIANCE EVER FORGED IN NATURE BETWEEN SUCH DIVERSE BEINGS. ”

• USA. Tough and characteristic in appearance, the Pinto has always been used to work with herds and in rodeos.

114 • Germany. Manes flying in the wind, three Irish Tinkers break into a gallop.

115 • Germany. The magnificent Irish Tinker is descended from horses selected by nomadic tinkers in Ireland.

Germany. Besides a dark complexion, Irish Tinker have spectacular long hair.

Germany. Because of its "square" structure, the Irish Tinker is an excellent workhorse, but it also has a docile and sensitive temperament.

120 ● USA. The Appaloosa is the classic "Western" horse, ideal for galloping, with plenty of speed and stamina. This type of coast is described as "marble."

121 ● USA. The Appaloosa's speckled coat gives this sturdy, vigorous and muscular horse a gentle complexion.

AMONG HORSES, THE INFINITE COMBINATIONS OF COLORS AND PAT-
TERNS OF THEIR COATS REFLECT FAR MORE THAN MERE AESTHETIC SURFACE
TRAITS. THIS IS BECAUSE THEY IDENTIFY NOT ONLY A BREED OF HORSES BUT A
DISTINCT PERSONALITY. REGARDLESS OF WHETHER IT IS AN ARABIAN OR NOR-
MAN, FRIESIAN OR APPALOOSA, THE HORSE IS AN INDIVIDUAL FIRST AND FORE-
MOST, WITH ITS OWN PERSONALITY AMONG THE OTHERS.

122 and 123 ● USA. The unique pattern on an Appaloosa's coat is a sort of identity card that makes it immediately identifiable.

124-125 ● Great Britain. Shire horses have distinctive long hair around their hocks.

126 ● Great Britain. Though taller, Shires resemble Friesians, a breed with which they were probably crossed in the Middle Ages.

127 ● Great Britain. Dark-haired Shire horses (whether black or bay) often have white patches.

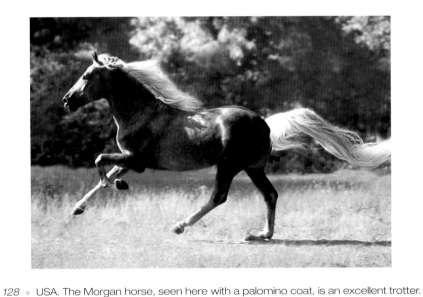

128 • USA. The Morgan horse, seen here with a palomino coat, is an excellent trotter.

129 • USA. A horse from the American "frontier" like the Appaloosa, the Morgan is extremely versatile, and can be ridden or used as a draft animal. It is also ideal for competitions and parades.

Great Britain. Two Shires at the gallop shine with sweat; note their huge and powerful muscles.

USA. Though particularly sensitive to sunlight, the American White is very vigorous and versatile. Muscular, with a broad chest and strong legs, American Whites have the characteristics of the breed's ancestor, Old King, who lived in the early 1900s.

134 • Great Britain. The Thoroughbred is a graceful and nimble horse made for galloping.

135 • Great Britain. An English Thoroughbred has an elegant, lean head.

WILD

in the

ATTILA KORBELY

INTRODUCTION Horses in the Wild

As far as looks go, horses display a stunning range of variation. Consider just a few examples: Shetland and Fjord ponies reminiscent of Disney cartoons; Friesian horses boasting majestic manes; massive draft horses; graceful thoroughbreds; wild mustangs – and the list could go on. But this was not always the case. The ancient horse hails from North America. Before vanishing from that continent, however, some horses crossed the Bering Strait and migrated to Asia, subsequently populating all of Eurasia. Humans began domesticating the horse approximately 5000 years ago, when the ancient horse probably exhibited a limited range of variation in

SHAPE AND COAT COLOR, DEPENDING ON HOW THE AN-
IMAL HAD ADJUSTED TO ITS HABITAT. TODAY'S DIVERSITY
IN SHAPE, COLOR AND SIZE IS LARGELY DUE TO HUMAN
INTERVENTION. THIS MAKES IT CLEAR WHY WE SHOULD
NOT REGARD FERAL HORSES – WHOSE ANCESTORS HAD
BEEN DOMESTIC HORSES – AS WILD HORSES. FORTU-
NATELY, THE ANCESTOR OF TODAY'S HORSES, THE ASIAT-
IC WILD HORSE, SURVIVES IN A SINGLE POPULATION THAT
LIVES ON THE STEPPES OF DZUNGARIA. AT THE END OF
THE 1960S, THIS POPULATION BECAME EXTINCT. FORTU-
NATELY, BY THEN A FEW SPECIMENS WERE IN EUROPEAN
ZOOS. EVENTUALLY, 11 ANIMALS WERE SELECTED FOR
BREEDING, AND DUE TO AN INTERNATIONAL PROGRAM
THE NUMBER OF WILD HORSES WAS BROUGHT BACK TO

INTRODUCTION Horses in the Wild

OVER 1500. THIS WAY, THE ASIATIC WILD HORSE (THE ON-
LY TRUE WILD HORSE SUBSPECIES TO SURVIVE) COULD BE
RETURNED TO ITS ORIGINAL HABITAT. THESE HORSES GO
BY SEVERAL NAMES – THEY ARE VARIOUSLY CALLED
PRZEWALSKI'S HORSE (NAMED AFTER THE RUSSIAN EX-
PLORER-NATURALIST WHO DISCOVERED THEM IN 1879),
TAKHI (THEIR MONGOLIAN NAME) AS WELL AS ASIATIC OR
MONGOLIAN WILD HORSE. THE ASIATIC WILD HORSE HAS
A DISTINCTIVE APPEARANCE – IT IS ZEBRA-LIKE IN ITS
MOVEMENT AS WELL AS APPEARANCE. BUT WHAT EX-
ACTLY ARE THE DIFFERENCES BETWEEN ASIATIC WILD
HORSES AND HORSES THAT WERE ONCE DOMESTICATED
AND ARE NOW FERAL? FIRST, WILD HORSES COME FROM
ANCESTORS THAT HAVE NEVER BEEN DOMESTICATED.

THEIR 'WILDNESS' IS DEFINED BY ANOTHER IMPORTANT ASPECT. HUMANS USUALLY HERD HORSES WITH THE HELP OF A DOG OR A WHIP DOG, BUT A WILD HORSE CAN ONLY BE HERDED BY OTHER WILD HORSES. WHEN A STALLION WITH A HAREM APPROACHES ANOTHER, HE HERDS HIS MARES AND FOALS WITH NECK AND HEAD HELD STIFFLY AHEAD, EARS FLATTENED. BUT THESE CHARACTERISTI-CALLY STUBBORN ANIMALS DO NOT TEND TO LIKE THIS KIND OF DISPLAY, AND THE HERD TRIES TO KEEP THE IN-TRUDING STALLION AT BAY BY BITING AND KICKING. HOLD-ING TOGETHER A LARGE HAREM TAKES VIGILANCE, PER-SISTENCE AND ENERGY. ASIATIC WILD HORSES LIVE IN SO-CIAL GROUPS OR SOMETIMES SOLITARILY. UNLIKE DOMES-TICATED AND FERAL HORSES, THEY ARE EXTREMELY AG-

GRESSIVE; A STALLION NOT ONLY PROTECTS ITS HAREM AND FOALS BUT SOMETIMES CONFRONTS OTHER HORSES FROM MILES AWAY TO FEND THEM OFF. THE WIND BRINGS A SHORT NEIGH ACROSS THE STEPPE. THE DOMINANT MALE LEAVES HIS HAREM AND CANTERS A FEW HUNDRED YARDS TOWARD THE SOURCE OF THE SOUND AND THEN STANDS STILL AND LISTENS WHILE FIXING HIS GAZE ON A SINGLE SPOT ON THE HORIZON. HIS HAREM GATHERS AROUND HIM, LOOKING WORRIED. IF NEITHER OF THE MALES BACKS OFF, THEN BOTH BEGIN FIERCELY TOSSING THEIR HEADS BACK AND FORTH, STAMPING ON THE GROUND WITH THEIR FRONT FEET, NEIGHING AND CALLING ON THE OTHER TO LEAVE. THEN, AS THOUGH THEY WERE PERFORMING AT A SPANISH RIDING SCHOOL,

Horses in the Wild
Introduction

THEY BEGIN A COLLECTED TROT TOWARD EACH OTHER ARCHING THEIR NECKS, EVENTUALLY JUMPING AT THE OTHER. THIS GESTURE IS JUST A SIMPLE SHOW OF POWER. WHEN THE STAKES ARE HIGHER, HOWEVER, AND A STALLION IS TRYING TO ACQUIRE A HAREM, THERE CAN BE BLOODSHED, SOMETIMES ENDING WITH THE DEATH OF ONE OF THE CONTENDERS. WILD HORSES HAVE A STRIKINGLY SWEET HABIT OF GROOMING: THEY STAND LANGUIDLY IN PAIRS, FACE TO FACE, FOR HOURS ON END, PECKING AND NIPPING AT EACH OTHER'S NECKS AND SIDES. DURING THIS "TEAM-BUILDING EXERCISE," AN AURA OF SERENITY DESCENDS OVER THE ANIMALS, MOMENTARILY OBSCURING THEIR WILD NATURE. . . .

145 ● France. A horse in the Camargue dashes across a ford in the Rhone delta.

146-147 ● France. The Rhone's chilly waters don't deter this playful herd.

● France.
Since most of the herds
of horses of the
Camargue roam freely,
they must move often to
find food in the poor
lands of the marshes of
the Rhone Delta.

● France. The horses of the Camargue, which are mainly gray in color, live semi-wild in the unique environment of the marshlands, to which they have adapted perfectly.

152 and 153 • France. Camargue horses graze amid the corn poppies of the French Midi.

154-155 • Portugal. Horses are free to gallop unimpeded on the plains of Portugal.

156-157 • USA. North Americas open spaces seem ideal for wild horses.

Iceland. Originally selected as mountain horses, Iceland ponies are completely at ease on rough terrain and have no trouble climbing the steepest slopes.

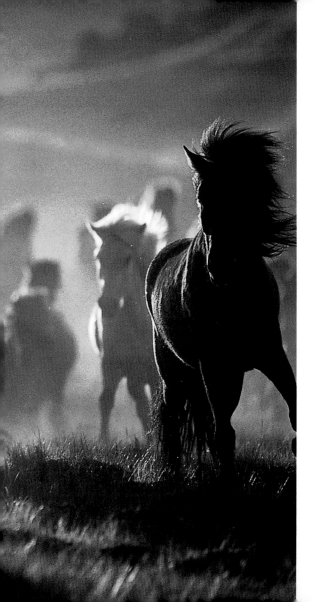

Iceland. Ponies in Iceland have an extra gait known as *tølt*; it consists of bringing both legs on one side forward at the same time.

Iceland. The moors and grasslands on Iceland's hills are home to half-wild herds of horses.

● Iceland. A line of ponies heads down a path in Iceland using the *tølt* gait.

166-167 • Russia. Originally from Mongolia, Przewalsky horses are also known as wild Asian horses, though now they have almost disappeared from the Mongolian prairies.

168-169 • Argentina. The permanently snow-covered Patagonian Andes provide an impressive backdrop for this cavalcade.

170-171 • USA. A group of twenty or twenty-five mustangs at the gallop during a North American winter.

Great Britain. Born virtually immune to the cold, these ponies seem to enjoy themselves on the snowy slopes of Scotland.

USA. Elegant and fast, Mustangs run free in the American prairies.

176-177 USA. A ford in South Dakota provides a chance to cool down and play.

178-179 USA. Headed by a herd leader, these wild horses cross a swollen river in South Dakota.

180-181 USA. Impetuous natures and harmony of movement: a group of Thoroughbreds against the big sky of Montana.

182-183 USA. Wyoming's long grass country encourages these colts and fillies in their instinctive tendency to run.

The FUTURE of the

SENIO SENSI

• France. This Arabian foal's sweet face shows the grace and beauty of this breed.

INTRODUCTION The Steeds of the Future

I HAVE ALWAYS THOUGHT THAT ANIMALS HAVE A SECRET LIFE THAT NOT EVEN ETHOLOGY CAN EXPLAIN. THEY HAVE A LIFE OF EMOTIONS, SENTIMENTS, SORROWS AND JOY PERHAPS EQUAL TO OUR OWN. THE INNERMOST SECRET LIES IN THE BIRTH OF AN ANIMAL: WHEREAS A WOMAN CAN EXPLAIN, ASK AND INFORM, UNLESS THEY LEAVE NATURE TO LOOK AFTER ITSELF, ANIMALS CAN ONLY LOOK AT US, ALMOST IMPLORINGLY, FOR SUPPORT. QUITE BY CHANCE, I WAS ONCE PRESENT AT THE BIRTH OF A FARM HORSE; NEEDING A BREECH DELIVERY, THE FOAL REQUIRED ALL THE EXPERIENCE, ENERGY AND DELICACY OF THE VET AND FARMER SO THAT IT WOULD NOT DIE DURING THE BIRTH. AS SOON AS THE PLACENTA DROPPED OUT

INTRODUCTION The Steeds of the Future

OF THE MOTHER'S BODY, SHE EXAMINED HER FOAL, AND SNIFFED AND LICKED IT. THE TINY NEWCOMER ATTEMPTED TO STAND UP BUT CLUMSILY FELL OVER. IT WAS MORE FORTUNATE A LITTLE LATER WHEN IT SEARCHED FOR ITS MOTHER'S TEAT AND BEGAN TO SUCK. GANGLING AND A LITTLE COMICAL, ITS LONG LEGS AND TINY BODY MADE IT RESEMBLE A BOY THAT HAD GROWN TOO QUICKLY. FOAL: THE OFFSPRING OF A HORSE. A TINY FOAL: THE DEFINITION OF TENDERNESS. FOALS SHOULD ALWAYS HAVE A CHILD CLOSE BY FOR RECIPROCAL BENEFIT: SO THAT THE CHILD WILL LEARN TO RESPECT ANIMALS AND THE FOAL WILL HAVE A LESS TRAUMATIC EXPERIENCE WHEN IT COMES TO BE TRAINED, AS, THOUGH THIS IS A STAN-

The Steeds of the Future

Introduction

DARD OCCURRENCE, IT IS AN UNNATURAL ONE. A FOAL IS THE SYMBOL OF JOYOUS FREEDOM. IT PLAYS IN ITS FIELD WITHOUT LOGIC OR RULES, THEN RE-TURNS TO ITS MOTHER TO LEARN AND IMITATE PROUDLY HER PHYSICAL MOVEMENTS. WATCHING A FOAL AND ITS MOTHER I SOMETIMES WONDER WHAT TYPE OF COMMUNICATION LINKS THE TWO OTHER THAN TEACHING BY EXAMPLE. TEACHING A YOUNG-STER HOW TO LIVE ITS LIFE IS DIFFICULT FOR ONE AND ALL, BUT MORE SO TO THOSE WHO ARE SUBJECTED TO THE DEMANDS OF MAN. PERHAPS THIS IS A SECRET THAT IT IS BETTER NOT TO FIND OUT.

France. An Arabian colt explores the world as he develops his independence.

190-191 ● Austria. A palomino-coated
Haflinger coat seems to draw a sense of
security from his mother's proximity.

191 ● France. While his mother feeds, the
small Arabian remains close by; he is
almost fearful.

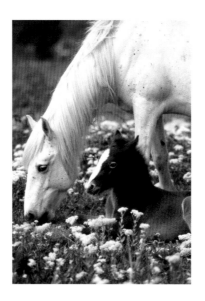

192 and 193 ● France. With its mother, the foal learns to distinguish edible herbs.

194-195 ● Great Britain. A tiny Shetland plays with his mother, helping to develop his muscles.

196 ● France. The mother-child bond is very strong among horses.

197 ● Asia. Mother and foal of the Przewalski breed in a pose of tender "complicity."

USA. Two foals rest happily in a soft, grassy meadow. A foal's life includes wild, scatty gallops and deep sleeps.

200-201 ● Iceland. This little Iceland pony doesn't seem to want to wander far from his mother.

201 ● Great Britain. A young Shetland pony comfortably asleep in a field.

202-203 ● Austria. The foals of many species – in this case a Haflinger – gradually lose the down they have when they are born.

Great Britain. Two colts play freely: moments like these help to teach them jumping movements.

Great Britain. A pair of foals frolics close to the adults of the herd; they gaze at each other, discovering the world around them together.

208 and 209 ● Germany. The first neighs of two very young foals: communication is fundamental in the animal world.

210-211 ● Iceland. This Iceland pony seems to be hiding behind his mother's reassuring bulk.

USA. A foal trots and then rests in a colorful field.

214 and 215 ● Great Britain. Foals need constant contact with the adults in the herd.

216-217 ● Germany. A Shetland pony adopts the most extreme – and comical –
way to scratch its back.

Germany. Two foals concentrate on cleaning themselves. Their sense of touch is so highly developed that even a fly landing anywhere on their body is enough to trigger a reaction.

220 ● USA. Long, slender legs, clearly out of proportion to their bodies, help foals move with a minimum of agility and speed.

221 ● France. An Appaloosa cares for and cleans his coat.

222 • Great Britain. A baby Gypsy Vanner stretches his legs in playful jumps next to an adult.

223 • Great Britain. A lovely dappled colt bucks energetically, its movements showing remarkable natural elegance.

Germany. A Friesian colt, already looking as haughty as an adult of the breed, stands near its mother.

Great Britain. On the left, an
Arabian looks at a kitten; on the
right, a Shetland pony curiously
watches an egret.

228 ● Great Britain. A tranquil trot for these colts that are familiarizing themselves with the world around them.

229 ● Ireland. The mother of a tiny Irish pony teaches her youngster to run in the open space.

THE CONDITION OF FOALS IS SINGULAR, AS THEY ARE THE GAWKY OFFSPRING OF WHAT WE PERCEIVE AS THE MOST GRACEFUL CREATURES ON EARTH. THIS MAKES THEM ALL THE MORE TOUCHING TO OBSERVE AS THEY DETERMINEDLY FOLLOW THEIR PARENTS' EXAMPLE TO FACE WHAT WE CAN EASILY DEFINE AS A METAMORPHOSIS RATHER THAN NORMAL GROWTH.

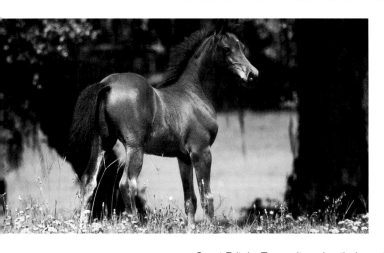

● Great Britain. Two colts enjoy their contact with nature in complete solitude.

232 ● Germany. There is a long tradition of breeding Arabian foals: the Bedouins considered them a priceless treasure.

233 ● Germany. Arabian foals show all the breed's sense of pride and elegance, but on a smaller scale.

Germany. A mother lavishes care and attention on her foal. As a rule, horses are extremely affectionate and sensitive: "friendly" in the full sense of the word.

Great Britain. An Arabian colt – a bay – is cared for by its gray-coated mother. The rarest color in the foals of this breed is all black.

USA. An Arabian foal suckles his mother. After the birth, a foal will normally be able to stand within an hour, and the first thing he does is to drink his mother's rich milk.

240-241 • Great Britain. A gray-coated Arabian lavishes attention on her bay foal. The rarest color for foals of this breed is all black.

242-243 • Great Britain. An entire family runs in the meadow: this is an excellent exercise for the growth of young foals and fillies.

244 ● Germany. Foals communicate on various levels. Even the position of their ears, erect and relaxed as here, is significant.

245 ● Germany. The sense of smell is the most important one in social relations among foals. As they smell, they often raise their upper lip slightly.

246 ● Great Britain. An Arabian colt seeks shelter under his mother's belly.

247 ● Germany. Ponies often turn to their mothers, as they seek their attention for something or simply want to run and frolic.

Iceland. A small Iceland pony tries every position imaginable to rest. Here, though the pony seems to be grazing, it is actually dozing.

WHINNIES and

GABRIELE BOISELLE

251 • Iceland. The Palomino pony almost looks angry. In reality, this kind of grimace is referred to as the Flehman reflex, and it is connected with olfactory perception.

253 • Austria. Haflingers are generally very gentle by nature but during the mating season aggressiveness and fighting is seen more frequently.

INTRODUCTION Muzzles and Whinnies

My PROFESSION AS A PHOTOGRAPHER BRINGS ME CLOSER TO MORE DIFFERENT TYPES OF HORSE THAN ALMOST ANYBODY ELSE CAN HOPE TO MEET. THERE ARE THE TIMID ONES AND THE RUDE ONES, THE ARROGANT ONES AND THE "MACHOS." I CAN NEVER TELL WHICH CHARACTER WILL POP UP IN FRONT OF MY LENS. AND I AM ALWAYS ANXIOUSLY LOOKING FORWARD TO DISCOVER GREAT NEW PERSONALITIES ON MY PHO-TO-SHOOTS – AND MOST OFTEN SUCCEED. SOMETIMES I REALLY HAVE TO WATCH OUT. ONCE I PHOTOGRAPHED ANSATA NILE PASCHA, A WELL-REGARDED CHAMPION ARABIAN STALLION. THIS VERY SPECIAL HORSE HAD SEEN IT ALL, ALL THE SHOW RINGS OF THE WORLD,

INTRODUCTION Muzzles and Whinnies

BOTH SIDES OF THE OCEAN IN AMERICA AND EUROPE. HE WAS JUST FED UP WITH ALL THE CRUELLY BURDEN- SOME DEMANDS OF THE TRAINERS AND WAS BEGGING TO BE A NORMAL HORSE OUT IN THE FIELD. BUT BEING TO VALUABLE HE HAD TO GO TO WORK AND HATED IT. AND HE HATED ALL THE PEOPLE WEARING DRESSED UP IN WHITE FOR A PERFORMANCE OR STRUTTING AROUND CARRYING A WHIP IN THEIR HANDS. UNFORTU- NATELY, THAT DAY I WAS IN WHITE WITH MY CAMERA IN MY HAND – AND THAT DID NOT LOOK GOOD TO THE STALLION. SO HE CAME TOWARD, EYES BLAZING, TEETH BARED. FOR A MOMENT, MY BREATHING FROZE; I KNEW I WOULD NOT BE FAST ENOUGH TO ESCAPE THROUGH THE FENCE. TRUSTING TO THE INSTINCTS I HAD DEVE-

INTRODUCTION Muzzles and Whinnies

LOPED WITH HORSES, I DID NOT WAIT UNTIL HE HAD REACHED ME, BUT SPRANG FORWARD TOWARD HIM LIKE AN ATTACKING FORCE. HE WAS SO TAKEN BY SUR-PRISE THAT HE JUMPED ASIDE, STOPPED AND TURNED AROUND WITH AN EXPRESSIONLESS FACE, ASKING "WHAT WAS THAT??? THEN HE CAREFULLY STEPPED CLOSER, AS IF ASKING "HALLO! WHO ARE YOU?" SO, I HAD BROKEN HIS BARRIER OF HATE. I PUT MY CAMERA ASIDE AND WE PLAYED AROUND FOR ABOUT HALF AN HOUR IN THE PASTURE – HE HAD FUN WITH ME. HE WAS ONE OF THE MOST PERFECT MODELS I HAVE EVER HAD AND AS GENTLE AND COOPERATING AS YOU COULD IMAGINE . . . SO LONG AS NONE OF HIS TRAINERS SHOWED UP. I'VE LEARNED ONE LESSON IN MY JOB:

Muzzles and Whinnies
Introduction

NEVER TRUST THE WORD OF PEOPLE ABOUT HORSES. YOU MUST YOURSELF DISCOVER THE MAKE-UP OF THE HORSE IN FRONT OF YOU: INSIDE AND OUTSIDE. AND I NEVER FOUND A REALLY MEAN HORSE THAT WAS NOT MADE MEAN BY MAN. HORSES ARE THE MOST NOBLE AND SPIRITUAL CREATURES I HAVE EVER MET IN MY LIFE. I HAVE SEEN HORSES BEATEN UP AND MISTREATED YET STILL FAITHFUL AND LOYAL. I HAVE SEEN HORSES CARING FOR THEIR HANDICAPPED RIDERS, LIKE FOR THEIR OWN CHILDREN. I AM BLESSED TO BE ABLE TO DISCOVER THE WORLD OF HORSES AGAIN AND AGAIN, TO LEARN SO MUCH ABOUT THEM – AND TO ADORE THEM MORE AND MORE.

Iceland. Iceland ponies being demonstrative. Horses are social animals and hate to be alone.

Argentina. Criollo stallions fiercely defending their mares. The winner will lead the entire herd.

● Argentina. Determined
and independent, Criollo
stallions have a very
strong character amply
demonstrated in their
"fiery" behavior.

Argentina. A Criollo
stallion demonstrates his
physical strength.

Germany. A bay and sorrel use their physical strength trying
to defeat one another.

Austria. Two Haflingers battle to win the leadership of the herd. In this struggle, each horse tries to defeat the other, using its robust jaws and kicking with its front legs in the attempt.

268 ● France. The bay clearly seems to have got the better of his adversary.

269 ● The Netherlands. Fighting between horses, Friesians in this case, may not be "to the death," but can nevertheless be violent.

270 ● Austria. A dramatic fight between two Haflinger ponies.

271 ● The Netherlands. A Friesian expresses the sheer joy of freedom with spontaneous enthusiasm.

272 ● Ireland. Gypsy Vanners are athletically built, which makes them well suited to riding and dressage.

272-273 ● Great Britain. Bred horses, in this case a Gypsy Vanner, need just as much freedom and open space as their wild cousins.

Iceland. Two Iceland ponies show their teeth in an act of defiance. If tamed early, this breed is very gentle.

France.
France. A horse from
the Camargue seems
to have relished its
meal. Wild horses eat
only a little at a time,
but often.

278-279 ● Egypt. An Arabian energetically scratches its back in the dust.

279 ● The Netherlands. A black Friesian finds relief from the insects by rolling on the ground.

Spain. Andalusian horses rub against a tree trunk. Regardless of where they live, horses must deal with an ever-present torment: insects.

● France.
France. A stockade
becomes a welcome
source of relief for this
wild horse tormented by
itchiness.

Italy. These horses behave tenderly toward each other during the courting season.

Spain.
Two Spanish horses
show affectionate
behavior. This breed, with
a noble appearance and
character, is very strong
and athletic and can be
tamed with great ease.

288 • Iceland. Two Iceland ponies seek contact with each other.

289 • Hungary. Shagya Arabians are tender towards one another.

Austria. Horses detest solitude, so they are often seen side by side in pairs, like these two Haflingers.

LIFE

on the RANCH

MEDFORD TAYLOR

• USA. A cowboy and his horse show off in a wild vault.

INTRODUCTION Life on the Ranch

"YEE HA! . . . HERE THEY COME." DISTANT HOOFBEATS BREAK THE DAWN ON ASSATEAGUE IS-LAND, VIRGINIA. SUDDENLY, FROM OUT OF THE FOG HANGING LOW OVER THE SALT MARSHES AND DUNES, HORSES APPEAR, POUNDING THEIR WAY ACROSS THE SAND. ON THIS JULY MORNING, "SALTWATER" COW-BOYS MOVE THE NORTHERN HERD OF WILD HORSES TOWARD THE OCEAN FOR A TWO-MILE TROT ALONG THE BEACH AND THEN THE CHANNEL SWIM TO CHIN-COTEAGUE. THIS IS THE START OF THE ANNUAL PONY PENNING. DURING ONE WEEK EVERY YEAR, A GROUP OF MEN FROM A VARIETY OF PROFESSIONS MEET UP FOR THE WILD HORSE ROUNDUP. AND FOR THIS BRIEF

• Italy. A Tuscan hand tends the herd.

INTRODUCTION Life on the Ranch

TIME IN SUMMER THEY BECOME SALTWATER COW-
BOYS, AND PARTICIPATE IN A TRADITIONAL ROUNDUP
THAT HAS LASTED FOR NEARLY 80 YEARS. 'I GREW UP
DREAMING OF BEING A COWBOY AND LOVING THE
COWBOY WAYS . . . PURSUING THE LIFE OF MY HIGH-
RIDING HEROES.' THESE WORDS, FROM THE WILLIE
NELSON SONG "MY HEROES HAVE ALWAYS BEEN COW-
BOYS," COULD BE THE DREAM OF EVERY BOY WHO
GREW UP GOING TO COWBOY MOVIES AS I DID. WEAR-
ING MY TOY SIX-GUNS, I WOULD RELIVE THE MOVIE ON
MY WALK BACK HOME FROM THE THEATER, IN THE
SOUTHERN TOWN WHERE I GREW UP. MANY YEARS
LATER AS A PHOTOGRAPHER ON ASSIGNMENT, I LAY
ON MY SWAG UNDER THE STARS OF THE AUSTRALIAN
OUTBACK . . . ON A REAL CATTLE MUSTER, WITH REAL

INTRODUCTION Life on the Ranch

COWBOYS . . . RINGERS, DOWN UNDER, MATE. I WAS AT PEACE . . . A BOYHOOD DREAM COME TRUE.

THE CREATION OF THE MYTHIC COWBOY PERSONA BY POPULAR CULTURE IS NOT CONFINED TO THE AMERICAN COWBOY – THE COWBOY IS A UNIVERSALLY ADMIRED LEGEND. IN MEXICO, HE'S CALLED VAQUERO. THE *GAUCHOS* OF ARGENTINA, URUGUAY AND BRAZIL STILL RIDE PROUDLY; ONCE CALLED THE 'WANDERERS OF THE PAMPAS,' *GAUCHOS* ARE A RESPECTED SYMBOL OF THEIR COUNTRIES HERITAGE. IN AUSTRALIA THE COWBOYS ARE RINGERS, JACKAROOS AND JILLAROOS, AND THEY LIVE AN INDEPENDENT AND RUGGED EXISTENCE. THE BUTTERO IS ITALY'S COWBOY. ALONG CENTRAL ITALY'S WESTERN BORDERS, IN TUSCANY, LIES THE HIDDEN FRONTIER OF MAREMMA. AN ALMOST

INTRODUCTION Life on the Ranch

MYTHICAL PLACE OF OPEN PLAINS AND FORESTS, MAREMMA IS HOME TO THE LAST OF THE BUTTERI. THERE ARE FEW WILD HORSES OR CATTLE LEFT, BUT MANY OF THE BUTTERI'S TRADITIONS ARE KEPT ALIVE THROUGH EVENTS SPONSORED BY BUTTERI D'ALTA MAREMMA, INCLUDING THE ANNUAL TRANSHUMANCE, A TWO-DAY WILD-HORSE ROUNDUP ACROSS THE TUS-CAN LANDSCAPE.

A COWBOY AND HIS HORSE ARE AS ONE. TOGETHER THEY DO A JOB. THEY WORK AS A TEAM THROUGH DRIVING RAIN, DUST STORMS, BLIZZARDS OR BAKING SUN. A COWBOY LOVES HIS HORSE BECAUSE HE IS LOYAL AND CARRIES HIM THROUGH THE BEST AND THE WORST OF TIMES, AND HE IS ALWAYS DILIGENT, NO MATTER HOW TIRED FROM HOURS UNDER THE SAD-

INTRODUCTION Life on the Ranch

DLE. A CENTURY AGO, A COWBOY AND HIS HORSE COULD RIDE THOUSANDS OF MILES ON ONE CATTLE DRIVE. TODAY THE AMERICAN WEST HAS BOUNDARIES, FENCES AND INTERSTATE HIGHWAYS. CATTLE ARE MOVED IN TERMS OF DAYS, NOT WEEKS OR MONTHS. IN AUSTRALIA, RINGERS NOW TAKE A FEW DAYS TO DRIVE CATTLE TO THE ROAD TRAINS, WHERE BEFORE IT WOULD TAKE WEEKS TO REACH A RAILHEAD. THE COWBOY'S WAY OF LIFE HAS CHANGED JUST LIKE EVERYONE ELSE'S. BUT FOR THE REST OF US, IT IS THE COWBOY'S WAY OF LIFE THAT WE ADMIRE. IT IS THEIR LIFE THAT WE ROMANTICIZE ABOUT, BECAUSE A COW-BOY REPRESENTS INDEPENDENCE, ADVENTURE AND WIDE OPEN SPACES. A VAQUERO, *GAUCHO*, BUTTERO, JACKAROO, OR BUCKAROO — THEY ARE PART OF

Life on the Ranch
Introduction

EACH COUNTRY'S HERITAGE, AND WE LOVE THEM FOR THEIR TENACITY TO SURVIVE IN CHANGING TIMES. BACK ON CHINCOTEAGUE, THE COLTS AND YEARLINGS HAVE BEEN SOLD AT AUCTION, AND THE SALTWATER COWBOYS DRIVE THE HORSES DOWN NARROW STREETS OF THIS ISLAND TOWN. THEY'RE HEADING BACK TO THE WATER TO SWIM THE CHANNEL HOME TO ASSATEAGUE ISLAND. WET COATS GLISTEN IN THE SUN AS THEY RISE FROM THE WATER AND THEIR HOOVES HIT FAMILIAR SAND AND MUD. WATCHING THE HORSES SHAKE THEIR MANES AND RUN FREE AGAIN YOU CAN ONLY HAVE A FEELING OF GRATITUDE, KNOWING THE HERD WILL STILL BE THERE NEXT YEAR WHEN THE SALTWATER COWBOYS RETURN.

- Argentina. Getting a herd across a river is a tough job: horses are delicate animals.

USA. Shoeing a horse requires skill and precision.

304-305 ● USA. The lasso is an everyday work tool for a cowboy.

305 ● USA. Keeping a herd of wild horses under control requires constant movement.

306-307 ● USA. Horses are led into the enclosure.

307 ● USA. The animals on a ranch are kept clean and healthy.

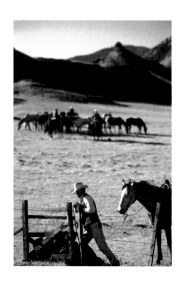

308 and 308-309 ● USA. Enclosure gates are made from simple poles that can be lifted out of the ground.

310-311 ● USA. Two cowboys break into a gallop in front of the mountains of Utah.

USA. A hand leads the herd as he loops his lasso in the air.

USA. A racing group of wild horses is a breathtaking sight.

316 ● USA. Boots and spurs are typical wear for cowboys.

316-317 ● USA. Other important pieces of clothing are suede leg protectors called chaps.

Canada. A blacksmith forges horseshoes in the semidarkness of his workshop. Life on the ranch follows age-old rhythms.

• USA. Horses are of major
importance in controlling herds
of cattle.

USA. Working with horses not only requires strength but also qualities such as sensitivity and awareness.

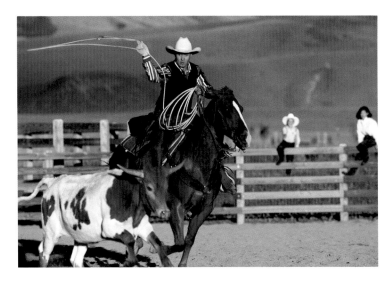

324 and 325 ● USA. In addition to being capable and courageous riders, cowboys must also be very agile and have great manual ability in order to handle the lasso correctly.

326-327 ● USA. A group of horses gallops freely outside the pen.

328-329 ● USA. The herd is checked every day, rain or shine.

340-341 ● USA. Wide open spaces and the open sky are appealing traits of the cowboy's work

from 342 to 345 ● USA. A vigilant eye needs to be kept when the herd is grazing or in the ring.

346 and 347 ● USA. Cowboys and horses have a hard time picking their way through the fresh snow. The Pinto, Quarterhorse and Appaloosa are the breeds preferred by cowboys because of their stamina and docile temperament.

348-349 ● USA. Cowboys have to handle the harshness of nature and the elements.

350-351 ● Argentina. Led by the *gaucho*, who is barely visible in the upper part of the picture, a herd of Criollos briskly fords a torrent on the pampa.

from 352 to 355 ●
Argentina. *Gauchos*
watch the herd from
behind for a better view.

Mexico. Lasso in hand to intimidate the cattle, the herdsmen rides along at the edge of the herd, close enough to keep it from dispersing.

358 ● Argentina. Criollos are difficult to train, and the presence of an already trained one often helps the process.

359 ● Argentina. Two *domadores* at work in the pen.

360-361 ● Argentina. The *domador*, who faces serious risks in his work, is a highly respected figure.

362-363 ● Argentina. Two *gauchos* recover a calf in difficulty.

363 and 364-365 ● Argentina. Fording rivers is a dramatic moment, often dangerous for men and horses.

366-367 ● Argentina. Two *gauchos* steer a herd of Criollos by whirling short crops called *rebenques*.

368 and 369 ● Italy. Tuscany's superb countryside is a fitting backdrop to these working herders.

370-371 ● Italy. Like other herdsmen around the world, the *butteri* work with horses every day, developing a very special rapport of equality and friendship.

FOR HERDSMEN AROUND THE WORLD AND THOSE WHO LIVE WITH LIVESTOCK EVERY DAY, THE HORSE MEANS WORK, FATIGUE AND SWEAT – RAIN OR SHINE – AND SLEEPING OUT IN THE OPEN. AT THE SAME TIME, HOWEVER, IT ALSO IMPLIES THE KIND OF FREEDOM DREAMED BY MANY AND ENJOYED BY FEW.

from 372 to 375 ● Italy. In the Maremma, the *butteri*'s horse is accustomed to living semi-wild in the country, alongside the longhorn cattle typical of the region.

Italy. The first step in training the Maremmana is handled without a saddle, working inside the pen.

378-379 ● France. The *gardians*, the herdsmen of the Camargue, follow a young bull. The cattle are raised in freedom in order to run during the traditional festivals of Provence.

380-381 ● France. A group of *gardians* precedes a large herd of cattle of the Camargue. The man in the middle grips the tool of this trade, the long handle of the *trident*.

Spain. A *doma vaqueras* follows the herd, which moves at rapid speed.

● Hungary. The thrilling spectacle of the *czikos*, the highly skilled Hungarian herdsmen, enlivens the *puszta*'s monotonous landscape.

● Hungary. A *czikos*, dressed in the traditional oversized blue shirt, guides a herd of magnificent bays across the *puszta*.

from 388 to 391 •
Mongolia. Mongolian
stockhands have to
brave very low
temperatures in wide
open spaces.

Australia. The Australian working cowboy's environment is usually huge, dry, dusty expanses.

394-395 ● Australia. A boat and cable are vital tools is bringing this horse across a broad river.

396-397 ● Australia. The cowboys' gait slows up to match that of their herds. It reflects the traditional – or "natural " – tempo of their calling.

Australia. Sun and dust accompany the herdsmen's daily work. In Australia, cowboys are referred to by various names, such as *jackaroos*, *jillaroos*, or *ringers*.

HORSES and

PAOLO MANILI

India. A very young Buddhist novice looks after a Mongolian horse.

INTRODUCTION Children and Horses

NOT ALL CHILDREN LIKE HORSES. SOME ARE FRIGHTENED OF THEIR SIZE OR, MORE SIMPLY, THEY PREFER OTHER ANIMALS LIKE DOGS, CATS AND RABBITS, ETC. ON THE OTHER HAND, THERE ARE CHILDREN WHO LIKE HORSES BEFORE THEY HAVE EVEN SEEN ONE. THIS ATTRACTION MAY RESULT FROM THEIR EDUCATION, CHILDREN'S STORIES, CARTOONS OR SIMPLY THEIR OWN CHARACTER. SUCH CHILDREN ARE EXTRAORDINARILY INTERESTED IN HORSES AND, WHEN THEY FIRST ENCOUNTER ONE, AN ALCHEMY OCCURS THAT NOT EVEN EXPERTS ARE ABLE TO DEFINE. THIS FASCINATION IS RETURNED BY HORSES THAT RECOGNIZE THAT THE YOUNG HUMANS BEFORE THEM ARE NOT PREDATORS TO FLEE BUT SIMPLY THE 'FOALS' OF ANOTHER SPECIES.

INTRODUCTION Children and Horses

IN ONE OF THE MYSTERIOUS LAWS OF NATURE, OFTEN EVEN SKITTISH HORSES ARE ATTENTIVE AND SHOW DELICACY TOWARD CHILDREN. THIS EXTRAORDINARY ANIMAL EXERTS A STRONG APPEAL ON PEOPLE, IN PARTICULAR THOSE WITH GREAT IMAGINATION: THE 'NOBLE QUADRUPED' CELEBRATED BY ARTISTS REPRESENTS BEAUTY AND GRACE, STRENGTH AND HUMAN DREAMS. THEY STIMULATE THE IMAGINATION, DESIRE AND THE DESIRE FOR POSSESSION. CHILDREN LOVE BEAUTY, THEY DREAM WITH OPEN EYES, WANTING THINGS THAT THEY LIKE. THEN, ONCE THEIR INTEREST IS RECIPROCATED, A LOVE SWELLS INSIDE THEM FOR THIS LARGE, APPRECIATIVE CREATURE, SO FRIENDLY THAT IT MIGHT BE A GIANT TOY. THIS SIMILARITY TO A TOY HAS BEEN TAKEN AS THE

Children and Horses

Introduction

BASIS FOR THE MOST RECENT METHOD OF TEACHING VERY YOUNG CHILDREN TO RIDE. IN COUNTRIES WHERE EQUESTRIANISM IS ADVANCED, CHILDREN START TO LEARN RIDING ON PONIES RATHER THAN HORSES FOR A MORE BALANCED RELATIONSHIP BETWEEN SIZE AND STRENGTH, AND THEY APPROACH COMPETITIVE RIDING THROUGH PONY GAMES. IN THE WEST PONY-RIDING COMPETITIONS ARE VERY COMMON AND EVEN HAVE AN INTERNATIONAL CALENDAR; THE BEST RIDERS ARE ELIGIBLE TO ENTER EUROPEAN AND WORLD CHAMPIONSHIPS IN VARIOUS DISCIPLINES AND ARE LIKELY TO GO ON TO BECOME FUTURE CHAMPIONS.

405 ● USA. A young rider carefully guides her pet to the ranch.

406-407 ● USA. A budding cowboy simulates a rodeo performance under the eyes of a 'real' cowboy.

408 ● USA. Whether made of wood or of real flesh and blood, a horse is a perfect play companion.

409 ● USA. Tackling the rudiments of lassoing.

410-411 ● USA. Before a rodeo, a young boy watches a horse with evident admiration.

USA. Youngsters together:
a boy and a colt gain confidence
as they study each other with
interest.

● Germany. A young rider shows her confidence in her magnificent Arabian. More than with other domesticated animals, human beings tend to treat horses as equals.

416 ● USA. An aspiring cowgirl in a matching outfit tenderly kisses her proud steed.

417 ● Ireland. A girl and a pony get to know one another. Horses love to be petted.

● USA. Once initial wariness is dissolved (mostly caused by the difference in size), children place complete trust in horses – a trust that will not be betrayed.

● Great Britain. The woolly shin-bones of a Shire are as tall as the squatting girl but she is not in any danger. Even the most skittish horses treat children with care.

422 • Great Britain. Two young jockeys jump a hedge during a competition.

423 • Great Britain. Falls are educational: a jockey slips from his saddle as he comes out of a jump.

424 ● Italy. An aspiring jockey dismounts, with some difficulty, from the saddle.

424-425 ● Great Britain. The enthusiasm of young riders – and their ponies – is unleashed at the gallop during a gymkhana.

426 ● Great Britain. Wearing a cap and
with her plaits in ribbons, a young girl
waits for the start of a competition.

426-427 ● Great Britain. Jumping with
style: learning is best done early.

428 and 429 ● Mongolia. Numbered participants at a horse-race in Mongolia prepare to start. The riders chosen are between 5 and 13 years of age because this ensures the ability of the horses is tested, not that of the riders.

430-431 ● Mongolia. Children and adults in the saddle of impressive young Mongolian horses accelerate into a gallop on the steppes.

UNIFORM

HENRY DALLAL

- Great Britain. On the Queen's Birthday, celebrated in June, the troops of the Household Cavalry (the Queen's personal guard) draw near to Windsor Castle.

INTRODUCTION Horses in Uniform

New to London, I was awakened by the echoing sounds of some thirty horses trotting in the cobblestone streets of this city. Running over to the window, the sight and the sounds of the "four-legged soldiers" with their mounted troopers on "watering orders" in the early morning darkness sparked fascination in me. Thus began my journey to photograph the Household Cavalry Mounted Regiment, the British Sovereign's Ceremonial Bodyguard, the elite of the world's mounted cavalry. Some 23,000 images later, with my book *PAGEANTRY AND PERFORMANCE* completed, I remained just as fascinated as when I first started this journey seven years ago. Britain is world-

INTRODUCTION Horses in Uniform

RENOWNED IN KEEPING ALIVE THE TRADITION OF THE WARHORSE OF YESTERYEAR IN ITS BRILLIANT POMP AND CEREMONY. WE HAVE THE HOUSEHOLD CAVALRY, THE KING'S TROOP ROYAL HORSE ARTILLERY, THE HONOURABLE ARTILLERY COMPANY, AND NUMEROUS OTHER UNITS, AS WELL AS THE ROYAL MEWS (STABLES) WITH ITS MUSEUM. SOME OTHER COUNTRIES ALSO MAINTAIN THE TRADITION OF THE "UNIFORMED HORSE," WEAVING IT IN THEIR CULTURE AND HISTORY. THERE IS THE GARDE REPUBLICAIN IN FRANCE, THE PRESIDENT'S BODY GUARD IN PAKISTAN, AND IN INDIA THE 61ST CAVALRY, AND IN CANADA THE ROYAL CANADIAN MOUNTED POLICE. THE CLOSER I LOOKED AT THE HORSE, THE MORE THERE WAS TO SEE AND MARVEL AT. BESIDES ITS SOFT VELVETY MUZZLE, EVERY

INTRODUCTION Horses in Uniform

HORSE HAS ITS INDIVIDUAL CHARACTER, PERSONALITY AND TEMPERAMENT. ON THE DAY OF AN EVENT SUCH AS THE QUEEN'S BIRTHDAY PARADE, AN 'ARMADA' OF OVER 400 HORSES COME TO DUTY AND TOGETHER WITH THEIR MOUNTED RIDERS (WHO AS MODERN SOLDIERS MAY HAVE JUST RETURNED FROM A BATTLE ZONE OR PEACE-KEEPING DUTY) RADIATE THAT GALLANTRY AND A SENSE OF PRIDE AND HONOR. EACH HORSE HAS BEEN TRAINED FOR MONTHS, AND ON THAT DAY, GROOMED FOR HOURS. THEIR HOOFS HAVE BEEN POLISHED; THE SOLES OF THEIR FEET POWDERED WITH WHITE CHALK. TROOPER AND HORSE ARE BRIGHTLY UNIFORMED WITH HEAVY SADDLES AND AC-COUTERMENTS, JUST AS IN DAYS OF CAVALRY BATTLES. THE CRISP EARLY MORNING LIGHT, THE MIST, THE HORSES'

INTRODUCTION Horses in Uniform

WARM BREATH VISIBLE IN THE AIR, ARE ALL PART OF THE EX-
PECTANCY. THE JINGLING AND CLANGING, AND THE OCCA-
SIONAL COUGH OR NEIGH AS THIS ARMY STANDS PATIENT-
LY IN RANK AND FILE WHILE THE COMMANDER INSPECTS
EVERY HORSE AND MOUNTED SOLDIER, BONDED AS ONE
PROUD BEING WAITING TO GO ON PARADE TO ESCORT THE
SOVEREIGN, PROUD TO STEP FORWARD AND MARCH IN
FRONT OF THE WORLD. WHETHER PULLING THE HEAVY
GUNS OR THE ROYAL COACH THEY KNOW THE ROUTE, THE
MOMENT, AND THE SOLEMNITY OF THE OCCASION. THERE
IS A TIME TO PLAY AND BUCK, AND THERE IS THE REQUIRE-
MENT TO STAND AT ATTENTION FOR HOURS. A COMPLETE
MOUNTED ORCHESTRA MARCHES PAST IN PERFECT STEP,
THE MUSICIANS OBEYING THE CONDUCTOR'S BATON AS HE

Horses in Uniform

Introduction

RIDES ON THE LEAD HORSE. THE HEAVY KETTLE DRUMS RE-VERBERATING WITH THE MUSIC'S BEAT, PLAYED BY A REINS-FREE DRUMMER, CAN BE IN A DIFFERENT TEMPO TO THE PACE OF THE MARCH. THROUGH THE LOUDLY CHEERING AND CLAPPING CROWD, BELOW THE HELICOPTERS CIR-CLING OVERHEAD, THE ARMADA OF NEARLY 400 HORSES PROUDLY PERFORM, MAINTAINING THE STRICTEST DISCI-PLINE. JUST OCCASIONALLY A PARTICULAR HORSE DE-CIDES, REGARDLESS OF HIS RIDERS RANK OR TITLE, HAS IT NO BUSINESS BEING IN THE ROYAL PROCESSION, AND THUS BEGINS HIS OWN SOLO PARADE, USUALLY AT A SWIFTER PACE AND IN A DIFFERENT DIRECTION, BUT EVENTUALLY TO THE PLACE WHERE HE IS FED. . . .

- Italy. The horseback band of the Carabinieri parade down Via dei Fori Imperiali in Rome.

Great Britain

440-441 ● Great Britain. The Life Guards here are seen walking in a circle at the end of the parade.

441 ● Great Britain. Roll-call for the Life Guards: the horses and their riders are subjected to an exhausting discipline.

442 ● Great Britain. A Horse Guard
awaits orders.

442-443 ● Great Britain. Saddles and
harness as splendid as on the days of
battle: everything must be perfect to
honor the royal household.

Great Britain. Tiny details, like the shine on the boots and stirrups, receive a maximum amount of attention. Note the regimental monogram inscribed on the hoof.

■ Great Britain. Wearing tunics embroidered with the Queen's monogram, musicians of the magnificent military band that accompanies the Trooping the Colour are able to play rhythms completely different to that of the march.

448-449 • Great Britain. The
Blues and Royals follow the Life
Guards out of Windsor Castle.

449 • Great Britain. Regiments
assemble in Windsor Castle's vast
Quadrangle.

Italy

- Italy. With the eternal Colosseum as a backdrop, the Carabinieri of the Cuirassier unit parade in Via dei Fori Imperiali during the Festa della Repubblica.

452 ● Italy. Drawn up in Piazza di Siena in Rome, the mounted Carabinieri await the start of the exciting Carosello.

453 ● Italy. Quadrilles of horseback Carabinieri perform changing formations during the Carosello, reproducing movements of troops in battle.

454-455 ● Italy. The Fanfara of the Carabinieri files past during the Festa della Repubblica in Rome.

● Italy. A company of
mounted Carabinieri break
into a gallop in the park at
Villa Borghese in Rome.

France

France. On July 14th, the festival that marks the fall of the Bastille, a sea of shiny helmets fills the Avenue des Champs Elysées. This is the Garde Republicaine on parade.

460 ● France. The gleaming helmet of this Garde Républicaine cavalryman reflects the French sky.

461 ● The Garde Républicaine's fanfare parades in front of the Louvre.

Spain

462 • Spain. A Spanish Civil Guard on service in the streets of Madrid.

462-463 • Spain. Horseback guards present their lances in Plaza de la Provincia in Madrid.

Sweden

464 ● Sweden. Trumpeters accompany the changing of the Swedish Royal Guards at the Royal Palace in Stockholm.

464-465 ● Sweden. The Swedish Royal Guard boasts the longest active service in the world: the regiment was formed in 1521.

Canada

466 ● Canada. Wearing red worsted jackets, lancers of the Mounted Police prepare for a Musical Ride, in which 32 officers perform complex figures on horseback to military band music.

467 ● Canada. Saddlecloths bear the monogram "MP", shorthand for the Royal Canadian Mounted Police.

● Canada. Units of horseback police (the famous Mounties) exhibit their skills at the gallop in a simulated charge in formation.

India

India. In New Delhi, units of the Presidential Guard maneuver in front of Rashtrapati Bhavan, the residence of the President of India.

from 472 to 475 ● India. Each year the Indian government invests large sums in the organization of the magnificent parades that celebrate the anniversary of the republic in the largest cities.

SPORTS

PAOLO MANILI

- Great Britain. Polo requires daring, speed and skill by both horses and riders.

INTRODUCTION Equestrian Sports

IT IS THANKS TO EQUESTRIAN SPORTS THAT HORSES HAVE SURVIVED THE ADVENT OF THE COMBUSTION ENGINE. WITH THE LESSENING OF THEIR FUNCTIONS AS A MEANS OF TRANSPORT AND A WORKING ANIMAL, THEY ONLY REMAIN IN USE IN ARMIES FOR TRAINING PURPOSES AND EXHIBITIONS. IT IS FROM CAVALRY EXERCISES THAT MODERN THREE-DAY 'EVENTING' IS DERIVED (ALSO KNOWN AS HORSE TRIALS, CONCOURS COMPLET, AND MILITARY COMPETITION). IN EVENTING, A HORSE IS PUT THROUGH THREE SEPARATE TRIALS ON CONSECUTIVE DAYS: DRESSAGE IN THE RING, A CROSS-COUNTRY ENDURANCE WITH JUMPS, AND SHOW JUMPING. EVENTING IS AN INDIVIDUAL

Switzerland. The White Turf is held each year in an unusual location for horseracing: the surface of the lake in St. Moritz.

OLYMPIC SPORT ALONG WITH DRESSAGE AND SHOW-JUMPING. THE FORMER, WHICH HAS ITS ORIGINS IN THE RIDING SCHOOLS OF THE 17TH AND 18TH CENTURIES, IS A DEMONSTRATION OF THE HORSE'S OBEDIENCE THROUGH A SERIES OF MOVEMENTS PERFORMED INSIDE A RECTANGLE OF PARTICULAR SIZE. SHOW-JUMPING HAS COMPETITIONS OF A DIFFERENT NATURE AND IS DERIVED FROM HUNTING: TO PROVE THE ABILITIES OF A HORSE, THE ANIMAL WAS MADE TO JUMP BARRIERS CONSTRUCTED TO RESEMBLE NATURAL OBSTACLES FOUND IN THE COUNTRYSIDE. IT WAS BUT A SHORT STEP FROM THIS TO THE ORGANIZATION OF COMPETITIONS. THE BASIS OF THE MODERN TECHNIQUE – WHICH WAS CODIFIED AT THE START OF THE 20TH CEN-

TURY BY CAPTAIN FEDERICO CAPRILLI OF THE ITALIAN CAVALRY AND INITIALLY TAUGHT AT THE PINEROLO SCHOOL – SPREAD AROUND THE WORLD. OTHER EQUESTRIAN SPECIALTIES ARE PRACTICED AT DIFFERENT LEVELS IN ALMOST ALL COUNTRIES, EACH WITH ITS OWN COMPETITION CALENDAR THAT INTEGRATES THE CONTINENTAL AND WORLD CHAMPIONSHIPS. FOR EXAMPLE, ENDURANCE RACES OVER DIFFERENT DISTANCES, ONE-, TWO- OR FOUR-HORSE HITCHES IN WHICH CARRIAGES ARE PULLED BY HORSES OVER COURSES TO DEMONSTRATE MANEUVERABILITY, AND VAULTING, IN WHICH A RIDER PERFORMS ARTISTIC AND GYMNASTIC MOVEMENTS WHILE THE HORSE IS MOVING IN A CIRCLE. THE LIST IS COMPLETED BY POLO, A SPORT

Equestrian Sports

Introduction

THAT ORIGINATED IN INDIA AND THAT THE BRITISH IM-PORTED TO EUROPE, AND HORSE-BALL, WHICH IS A SORT OF FOOTBALL ON HORSEBACK. THE OTHER HALF OF THE EQUESTRIAN UNIVERSE IS REPRESENTED BY WESTERN RIDING, INCLUDING CONTESTS THAT SIMU-LATE WORK SITUATIONS, LIKE ROUNDING UP CATTLE ON HORSEBACK. FROM THEIR ORIGIN AMONG THE NOBILI-TY AND ELITE, EQUESTRIAN SPORTS HAVE BECOME IN-CREASINGLY POPULAR AND WIDESPREAD, AND THUS GIVEN A BOOST TO THE IMPROVEMENT OF HORSE-BREEDING. RIDING IS ALSO A VERY 'MODERN' SPORT IN WHICH MEN AND WOMEN COMPETE TOGETHER, WITH THE LATTER OFTEN TAKING THE PRIZES.

The Netherlands. Approaching the fence, horse and rider are in total harmony.

Showjumping

484 • The Netherlands. At the 'top' of the jump, the horse seems suspended in the air.

485 • Sweden. As the horse leaves the ground, the rider thrusts his weight forward to assist his mount in the jump.

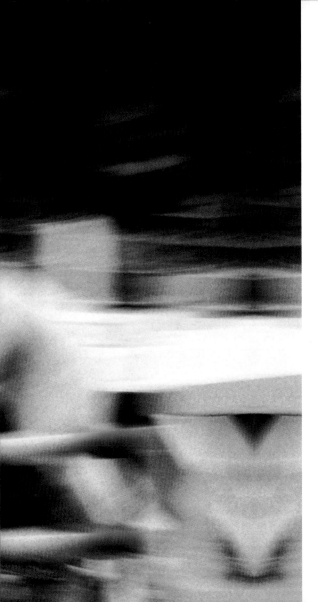

● Ireland. Once the jump is under way, the rest is up to the horse; the rider can no longer use the reins or whip to guide his mount.

488 ● Ireland. Landing is the most difficult phase for the rider, and it is easy to lose balance and fall.

489 ● Ireland. A 'messy' jump; the front legs are gathered unevenly toward the chest.

Scotland. The horse counts on its rider to manage the jump: the least uncertainty in the approach or on the rider's part and the horse refuses the jump.

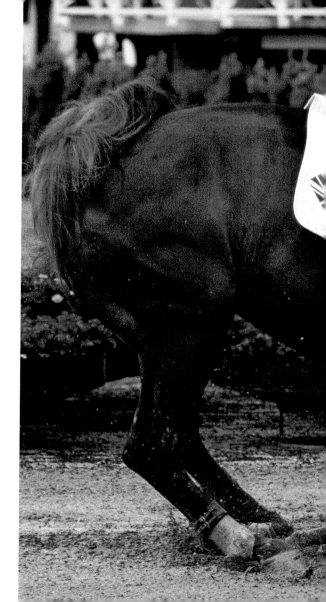

from 492 to 495 •
Spain and Great Britain.
The fall of the horse, rider
or both usually carries a
heavy penalty and, in
certain competitions,
elimination.

Dressage

496 • Spain. During the diagonal, the horse moves between opposite corners of the arena.

496-497 • Spain. Elegance, balance, naturalness and perfect understanding: dressage is one of the noblest equestrian disciplines, as shown here.

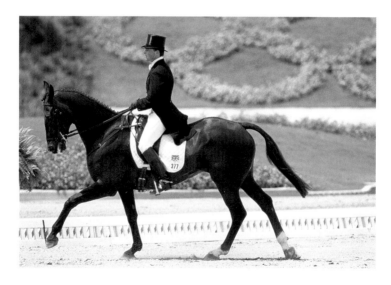

498 ● Australia. At a walking pace, the horse moves with a measured but powerful gait.

499 ● Australia. Communication between horse and rider passes through the bit: the connection between the hands of the rider and the mouth of the horse is called 'contact.'

Australia. A strong emotional bond unites rider and horse. At the end of an Olympic dressage competition, a rider compliments her horse with a caress.

● Spain. Words and physical contact
establish the fellowship required to
attempt a dressage competition.

Polo

Switzerland. In the spectacular snow polo matches, players use a red ball, much larger than the traditional white ball.

● Switzerland. The famous Cartier Polo World Cup is held in late January on the frozen surface of the St. Moritz lake.

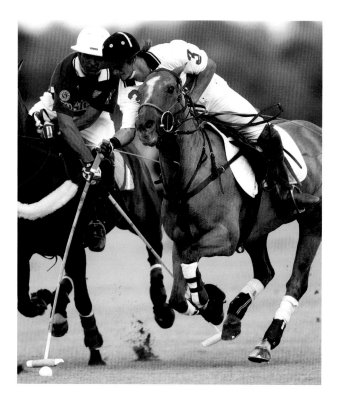

Great Britain. Polo mallets are made from flexible malacca wood and are approximately 52 inches long.

510-511 ● USA. Polo horses have to have strong hocks to deal with the physical strain: often the animals are ponies rather than horses.

512-513 ● Great Britain. To prevent dangerous collisions in polo, complex rights govern precedence.

from 514 to 517 • USA. Given the forcefulness of the game, hocks and shins are protected by pads to prevent excessive impact, but tails are also tied up to stop them getting tangled.

Trial

USA. The demanding Horse Trials are held over varied terrain with both artificial and natural obstacles, often with water.

Great Britain. Dramatic falls are not rare in Horse Trials.

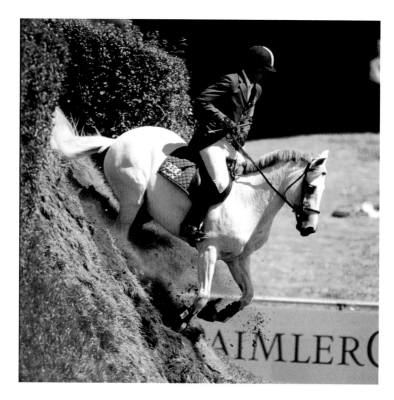

Great Britain. Dealing with embankments requires great power going up and total control of the horse coming back down.

Great Britain. Frequent
falls require that the
horses' legs are well
protected with padding
and special ointments.

Great Britain. As the pair are racing against the clock, Horse Trials are based on speed rather than style.

Harness

● Great Britain. Harness
racing includes different
categories: singles, pairs,
tandem driving (two
horses in a row) and, as
shown here, fours.

530-531 and 531 ● Great Britain.
At harnesses races there is a delightful
air of yesteryear.

532-533 ● Great Britain. In singles
driving, with a jockey and assistant,
notable speeds can be reached.

Trotting

from 534 to 541 •
Switzerland, Austria,
USA. Drivers in harness
racing or trotting races
sit in small, very light
metal gigs with rubber-
tired wheels known as
sulkies.

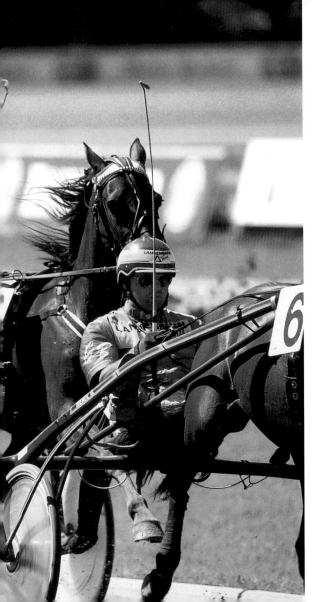

USA. The public identify competitors in harness racing by the colors the drivers wear.

Steeplechase

from 544 to 549 • Great Britain, Ireland. Steeplechasers require exceptional strength to tackle races over distances of 3,000 meters, jumping hedges, walls and ditches.

● Great Britain, Ireland. Because
steeplechase jumps cannot be moved,
riders sometimes have to take 'to the air.'

Racing

from 552 to 555
Switzerland. A rider at full
gallop flies out of a cloud
of snow. This is the White
Turf in St. Moritz, a
sporting event that
combines international
trotting and galloping
races.

from 556 to 559 • USA. Gates are needed to keep the chafing runners in line and apart. The instant they open, the horses unleash all their power in surging forward.

560-561 • USA. Speed is not everything in a race. Depending on individual characteristics, there are 'fast' and 'slow'; horses: it is strategy not speed alone that wins races.

USA. Similar to the blasons of medieval riders, the colors the jockeys wear identify the horses' owners.

564-565 ● Spain.
Pineda race track in
Seville resounds to the
thunder of hooves.

566-567 ● China.
Saddle and harness are
reduced to the minimum
so the horses carry the
lightest weight possible.

568 • Australia. This is the lead group in the Great Metropolitan Stakes in Randwick, Sydney, where races have been held since 1866.

569 • Australia. Racehorses begin their training at the age of two. The best are soon entered in races, others begin at up to five years of age.

Great Bretain. Given the high speed on the track and flying divots of turf, jockeys wear goggles. Ventilation holes at the sides prevent the problem of fogging up.

572 ● Ireland. The Galway Races have been held since the 13th century.

572-573 ● Australia. To assist the horse's movements, the jockey leans forward, seldom in contact with the saddle.

574-575 ● Ireland. Horses exhibit their full power in the gallop.

576-577 ● USA. The public loves horseracing because of the beauty of horses at full gallop.

Canada, Great Britain. Winners: a kiss for the horse is a demonstration of gratitude and affection.

The MAJOR SCHOOLS

PAOLO MANILI

- France. An instructor at the Cadre Noir School in Saumur, wearing a kepi and black uniform, directs a horse in a spectacular *cabriole*.

INTRODUCTION The Major Schools

IN *HIPPARCHIKOS* ('CAVALRY OFFICER') WRITTEN IN 362 BC, XENOPHON REFERRED TO 'SCHOOL WORK' WHICH INVESTIGATED HARMONY OF MOVEMENT IN THE GAIT OF A HORSE. RIDING METHODS TAUGHT DURING THE RENAISSANCE TENDED TO EMPHASIZE EXECUTION OF MOVEMENTS BECAUSE AT THAT TIME FIREARMS HAD MADE ARMOR OBSOLETE AND THEREFORE GREATER MANEUVERABILITY WAS REQUIRED FROM HORSES. SINCE THEN, UP TILL THE PRESENT DAY RIDING HAS EVOLVED FROM THAT DEVELOPMENT. IN THE 16TH CENTURY RIDING WAS A 'CONSTRICTIVE' ACTIVITY, AT TIMES BRUTAL (LIKE THAT OF FEDERICO GRISONE, A PUPIL OF GIOVANBAT-

Austria. Like a flesh-and-blood equestrian monument, a Lipizzaner performs a *courbette* at the Spanish Riding School in Vienna.

INTRODUCTION The Major Schools

TISTA PIGNATELLI, WHO WAS MASTER OF THE RIDING SCHOOL OF NAPLES) DUE TO THE HEAVY AND 'COLD' TYPE OF HORSES USED. HOWEVER, THE EQUESTRIAN ARTS GRADUALLY INCREASED THE STYLIZATION OF THE MOVEMENTS OF A HORSE IN BATTLE UNTIL THEY DEVEL-OPED INTO THE REFINED MOVEMENTS TAUGHT TODAY IN RIDING SCHOOLS. DRESSAGE WAS EXALTED IN THE HIGH SCHOOL WHICH LED, IN THE 17TH CENTURY, TO THE HIGHLY REFINED TECHNIQUES PRACTICED BY PLUVINEL AND NEWCASTLE. FRANÇOIS ROBICHON DE LA GUERINIÈRE (1687–1751), THE FATHER OF FRENCH EQUES-TRIANISM, TOOK RIDING TO THE FIRST, INCISIVE REVOLU-TION, ONE THAT ATTEMPTED TO MEDIATE RIDING VIRTU-OSITY WITH PRACTICALITY IN THE USE OF A HORSE. AFTER

INTRODUCTION The Major Schools

HIM, ACADEMIC RIDING CONTINUED TO DEVELOP UNTIL THE 19TH CENTURY WHILE HISTORICAL EVENTS DEMANDED A MORE VERSATILE USE OF SADDLE HORSES. AT THE START OF THE 20TH CENTURY, FEDERICO CAPRILLI (1868–1907), A CAPTAIN IN THE ITALIAN CAVALRY, CODIFIED THE 'NATURAL SYSTEM OF RIDING,' IN WHICH THE RIDER HAD TO ADAPT HIMSELF TO THE NATURAL BALANCES EXISTING IN THE HORSE'S GAIT RATHER THAN VICE VERSA. THIS WAS THE SECOND AND MORE FAR-REACHING REVOLUTION TO TAKE PLACE IN EQUESTRIANISM AND BECAME THE BASIS FOR MODERN RIDING TECHNIQUES. TAUGHT BY THE SCHOOL OF PINEROLO AND SOON SPREAD AROUND THE WORLD, PARTICULARLY WITH REGARD TO JUMPING, IT DISPENSED WITH THE STANDARD

The Major Schools

Introduction

RIDING TECHNIQUES TAUGHT. HOWEVER, SOME TRADI-
TIONAL SCHOOLS HAVE SURVIVED TO THE PRESENT, FOR
EXAMPLE THE SPANISH SCHOOL IN VIENNA (FOUNDED IN
1792 BY CHARLES V HABSBURG) AND THE SAUMUR
SCHOOL IN FRANCE (FOUNDED IN THE MID-18TH CENTU-
RY BY THE DUKE OF CHOISEUL). BOTH ARE 'SHRINES' TO
HORSE RIDING AND REPRESENT AN INESTIMABLE TECH-
NICAL AND CULTURAL VALUE. IN ORDER THAT SPANISH
TRADITIONS MIGHT BE PRESERVED, IN 1987 THE REAL ES-
CUELA ANDALUZA DEL ARTE EQUESTRE WAS FOUNDED
IN JEREZ DE LA FRONTERA IN ANDALUSIA BY ALVARO
DOMECQ ROMERO. THESE THREE ACADEMIES REPRE-
SENT THE HISTORY OF HORSE RIDING.

- France. The name "Cadre Noir," applied to the Saumur school's officials, was later applied to the school itself. It comes from the color of the instructors' uniform.

LEAPING HORSES THAT CREATE FLESH-AND-BLOOD EQUESTRIAN MONUMENTS, HORSES THAT BUCK AND REAR WITH A SENSE OF ART AND PROPORTION, HORSES THAT DANCE: IT TAKES DISCIPLINE TO DO ALL THIS. AT THE TEMPLES OF THE ART OF RIDING, HOWEVER, MAN AND HORSE LEARN TOGETHER, AND IT IS THE FORMER WHO MUST ADAPT TO THE LATTER.

● Spain. An enthralling sequence in a *cabriole* in four consecutive photographs: only horses with perfectly trained rear muscles are capable of this exercise.

France. In the culminating phase of the *cabriole*, the horse, which is completely off the ground, kicks vigorously backwards.

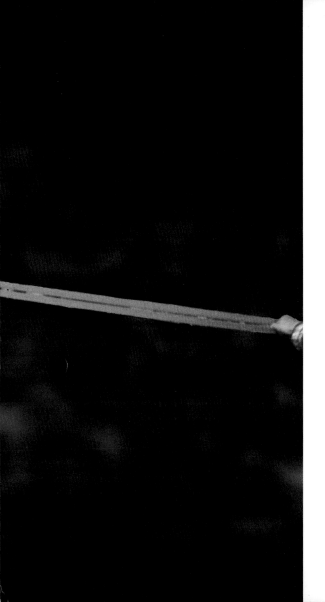

France. The *croupade* is part of the so-called *Arie Alte*, i.e., the figures in which the horse lifts all four legs at the same time.

Real Escuela Andaluza del Arte Equestre

Jerez (Spain)

• Spain. Trainers at work at the Real Escuela Andaluza del Arte Ecuestre in Jerez de la Frontera: the renowned school's pride is the exhibition of How Andalusian Horses Dance, which leaves no doubt as to the excellence of the art practiced here.

596 • Spain. The covered ring of the Picadero in Jerez de la Frontera is where the Real Escuela Andaluza del Arte Ecuestre has given its performances since 1987.

597 • Spain. With its front legs high against its chest, a horse executes a *courbette*, a figure in which the animal makes small jumps forward balancing only on its hind legs.

Le Cadre Noir
in Saumur
France

● France. The 'career' of the Cadre Noir horses (shown here in a *croupade* and a *courbette*) lasts only about 15 years; they are then sold to other schools, breeders or private individuals.

France. An elegant croupade at the Cadre Noir in Saumur. At the rider's command, the horse 'bucks', extending its rear legs completely.

602 and 603 • France. An instructor at the school in Saumur uses a long rein while training a horse to perform the *cabriole*.

604-605 • France. In the Cadre Noir riding school, two groups of five horses execute a *croupade* in sequence.

Spanische
Reitschule Vienna
Austria

from 606 to 611 ● Austria. Most of the magnificent and highly trained horses at the Spanish Riding School in Vienna (Spanische Reitschule) are Lipizzaners.

PARADE on

SENIO SENSI

- New Zealand. A rodeo contestant shows skill and a sense of acrobatics in the saddle on an untamed horse.

INTRODUCTION Horses on Parade

THE LOVE FELT FOR HORSES IS SHOWN IN MANY PARTS OF THE WORLD BY THEIR MAJOR ROLE IN OUTSTANDING NATIONAL EVENTS AND CELEBRATIONS. WHETHER IT'S PARADES AND REVIEWS, MEDIEVAL PROCESSIONS, OR RACING, CULTURAL AND RECRE-ATIONAL EVENTS, HORSES BRING SPLENDOR AND HONOR TO THEM WITH THEIR REGAL BEARING AND ABUNDANT ENERGY. FROM THE VIOLENT TWO- AND FOUR-HORSE CHARIOT RACES THAT ROUSED AUDI-ENCES IN ANCIENT ROME'S CIRCUSES, TO THE "RO-MANTIC" TOURNAMENTS OF THE MIDDLE AGES, IN WHICH MAGNIFICENTLY ARMORED AND CAPARISONED HORSES SHARED THE GLORY WITH DUELING KNIGHTS,

● Italy. Since 1644, the year it was first run, Siena's Palio has been a major event for the citizens.

AND FROM POLO, PLAYED IN PERSIA OVER 1,000 YEARS AGO, TO PATO, A SORT OF HORSE-BORNE BASKETBALL INVENTED IN ARGENTINA AROUND 1600, HORSES HAVE BEEN INDISPENSABLE TO MANY TYPES OF RECREATION.

THEN THERE ARE RECENTLY INVENTED WESTERN COMPETITIONS LIKE BARREL RACING (A RACE BASED PRIMARILY ON SPEED AROUND A COURSE MARKED BY THREE BARRELS INSIDE A CORRAL), POLE BENDING (LIKE AN "EQUESTRIAN SLALOM" THROUGH A COURSE MARKED BY SEVEN POLES), AND OF COURSE THE FAMOUS AND TRADITIONAL RODEOS, IN WHICH COWBOYS ATTEMPT TO RIDE WILD HORSES.

EUROPE HAS SEVERAL EQUIVALENTS OF THE AMERI-

CAN COWBOYS: THE *CSIKOS*, OR HUNGARIAN STOCK-MEN, WHO PERFORM AMAZING STUNTS ON HORSE-BACK AT LOCAL SHOWS AND FAIRS, THE *GARDIENS* OF THE CAMARGUE, WHO ANNUALLY PARADE ON HORSE-BACK THROUGH THE STREETS OF ARLES DURING THE *FÊTE DES GARDIENS*, AND THE ITALIAN *BUTTERI*, WHO SHOW OFF THEIR RIDING SKILLS AT TRADITIONAL EVENTS LIKE THE MERCA IN MONTEROMANO, A FAIR THAT FOCUSES ON CATTLE BRANDING. THEN TOO, MENTION MUST BE MADE OF THE FAMOUS HORSE RACES ON SNOW AT ST. MORITZ IN SWITZERLAND, IN-AUGURATED IN 1984 AND SOON COPIED IN SIMILAR COMPETITIONS IN LECH (AUSTRIA) AND MÉGÈVE (FRANCE), AND THE FANTASIES IN MOROCCO, THE

INTRODUCTION Horses on Parade

MOST IMPORTANT OF WHICH IS HELD IN HONOR OF IDRIS I (THE FATHER OF THE NATION). AS EVENING FALLS, A MULTICOLORED CAVALRY SIMULATES A CHARGE, FIRING LONG-BARRELED, DECORATED AND SILVER-CHASED RIFLES INTO THE AIR. IN SPAIN HORSES TAKE PART IN LONG ESTABLISHED EVENTS: IN SEVILLE, FOR EXAMPLE, DURING THE FERIA IN APRIL, THE CITY FILLS WITH HORSES DECKED OUT IN FINE TRAPPINGS AND RIDERS IN THE TRADITIONAL COSTUME OF THE ANDALUSIAN FAIR, BOTH EQUALLY PROUD. AND IN MAY IN JEREZ THE FERIA DEL CABALLO IS THE FAVORITE OCCASION OF HORSE ENTHUSIASTS. THE CITY CAN ALSO BOAST THE REAL ESCUELA ANDALUZA DE ARTE ECUESTRE DI JEREZ, ONE OF THE

INTRODUCTION Horses on Parade

MOST RENOWNED RIDING SCHOOLS IN THE WORLD. IN ITALY THE SARTIGLIA OF ORISTANO HAS BEEN FAMOUS SINCE 1543; THIS IS A PARADE OF CAPARISONED HORSES RIDDEN BY MASKED HORSEMEN PERFORMING ELEGANT MANEUVERS.

BUT SURELY THE PERFECT COMBINATION OF MAN AND MOUNT TAKES PLACE IN SIENA AT THE PALIO. THIS EVENT IS A RACE OF THREE LAPS AROUND THE PIAZZA DEL CAMPO IN WHICH THE WINNER IS CONSIDERED TO BE THE HORSE, NOT THE RIDER. IN FACT, THE HORSE IS ABLE TO TAKE HIS CONTRADA (CITY QUARTER) TO VICTORY EVEN IF HIS RIDER HAS BEEN UNSEATED.

BEFORE THE RACE THE HORSES ARE BLESSED IN CHURCH AND, IN THE EVENT OF VICTORY, IS SEATED AT

Horses on Parade

THE HEAD OF THE TABLE DURING THE CELEBRATORY FEAST THAT FOLLOWS. WATCHED OVER NIGHT AND DAY, THE HORSES UNLEASH THEIR NERVOUS ENERGY ON THE PIAZZA DEL CAMPO WHERE THEIR SAFETY AND WELL-BEING ARE GREATER THAN ANYWHERE ELSE IN THE WORLD.

WHEN THEY REACH OLD AGE, THEY ARE PENSIONED OFF IN A MEADOW AND, ON THEIR DEATH, THEY OFTEN RECEIVE THE TRIBUTE OF A TOMB AND DEATH NOTICE THAT DESCRIBES THEIR RACING PROWESS. IF I WERE A HORSE, I WOULD WANT TO RACE IN THE PALIO IN SIENA. AND I'M NOT THE ONLY ONE.

• Afghanistan. In a wild whirlwind of dust, a horde of riders attempts to win a goat. This is *Buskashi*, the Afghani national sport that boasts ancient origins.

Feria de Abril

Seville - Spain

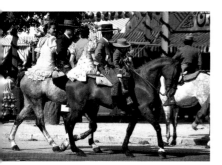

622 ● Spain. During the Fería de Abril in Seville, the bright colors of flamenco costume offset the glossy coats of the horses.

622-623 ● Spain. Man and horse become a single unit when expressing Andalusian pride.

Spain. During the Fería in Seville, the horses' heads are adorned with floral ornaments.

Spain. On the first day of the Fería, which begins the week after Easter, participants arrive in the city on horseback or on carts pulled by twosomes or foursomes.

from 628 to 631 • Spain. During the Feria de Abril, the gestures, poses and garb of a romantic and not-so-distant past are revived with powerful spontaneity.

Feria de Jerez

Jerez de la Frontera, Spain

632 and 633 • Spain. Horses' tails embellished with bright ribbons: the decorations worn by the riders blend with the beauty of the animals at the Fería in Jerez.

from 634 to 637 • Spain. The parade of the horses and carriages in the ring is a highlight of the Fería.

Fiesta de San Juan
Minorca - Spain

Spain. At the Fiesta di San Juan, which takes place in the streets of Minorca's old Muslim quarter, the horses move fearlessly through the crowd.

Spain. The king of the Fiesta is the Minorcan horse, appreciated for vigor coupled with ridability.

Spain. During the Fiesta, the horses change their gaits in response to their riders' orders.

Luminarias
San Bartolomé de los Pinares
Spain

Spain. A rider faces the flames with his horse, symbolically purifying the animal during the *Festival Luminarias* at San Bartolomé de los Pinares, in the province of Avila.

● Spain. The *Luminarias* festival is a
religious celebration held on the night
before St. Anthony's day, the patron saint
of animals.

Palio di Siena
Italy

Italy. The Palio di Siena
always arouses high
excitement in the riders,
the horses and the public.

Italy. Conveyed back to the height of the Middle Ages in the scene in the Piazza del Campo, the electrified audience follows the horserace. The event acquires an even more spectacular air as the pounding hooves throw up enveloping clouds of ocher earth.

Italy. During the Palio, the horses absolutely maximize their strength and stamina.

Sartiglia
di Oristano
Italy

Italy. The Sartiglia di Oristano is a joust instituted in 1543 to control the bloody clashes that took place between the Arborensi and Aragonesi.

Italy. In the *sartiglia* in Oristano (a game of Arabian-Iberian origin), riders perform a series of difficult exercises before the crowd.

Italy. The riders in Oristano perform acrobatic tricks like the human pyramid, the 'bridge' or the 'laterali in piedi.'

Oswald von Wolkenstein Ritt

Italy

● Italy. The Ride (Ritt) of Oswald von Wolkenstein, named after the celebrated mediaeval troubadour who lived here, is an event with games on horseback. It is held every June on the Sciliar Plateau.

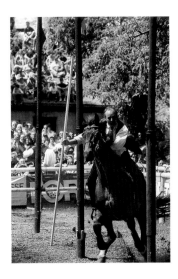

Italy. A set course includes games and tournaments that require ability, speed and precision.

Italy. Rider and horse must work in perfect harmony to be able to deal with the narrow spaces of each obstacle.

Puzta horsemen
Hungary

from 666 to 669
Hungary. During the equestrian events held on the *puszta*, the *czikos* – Magyar cowboys – show off with daredevil and dramatic acrobatics.

Ride of the Kings

Czech Republic

● Czech Republic. Once widespread throughout Moravia, today the Ride of the Kings is held only in the village of Vlcnov. During the festivities, which are part of the Easter celebrations, the horses' manes and coats are decorated with multicolor ribbons.

672-673 ● Czech Republic.
A triumph of colors accompanies
the King, in the center, escorted by
two horsemen.

673 ● Czech Republic. Damsels
dressed in the rich traditional
costumes of Vlcnov participate in
the Ride of the Kings.

Fantasia

Morocco

674 and 675 • Morocco. Fantasia are ceremonial simulations of a cavalry charge, symbolized by the shots fired into the air.

from 676 to 679 • Morocco. Fantasia is an opportunity to revive warrior traditions as well as a patriotic sense of belonging.

Durbar Festival

Nigeria

Nigeria. The celebrations of the Durbar Festival start at the end of Ramadan. The parade features fast-paced riding, in which participants raise their lances and swords to the sky.

682-683 ● Nigeria. The dark faces of the men blend with the black coats of the horses, thereby emphasizing the colors of the garments.

683 ● Nigeria. Nigerian and Berber ponies, which are small, agile and docile horses, play a starring role in the Durbar Festival.

Buskashi

Afghanistan

684 and 685 • Afghanistan. The *Buskashi* is the Afghan national sport; it is a horseback struggle to win the body of a decapitated goat.

686-687 ● Afghanistan. The *Buskashi* is not really a team game. The aim is simply to better everybody else.

Afghanistan. Violence plays a central role in trying to get possession of the goat's carcass, or what remains of it at the end of the contest.

Litang
Festival
China

from 690 to 693 China. Each year on Litang plateau in Tibet, thousands of people meet to challenge one another in tests of skill on horseback.

China. The participants in the Litang festival are from a tribe that was once composed of ferocious warriors. Today this legacy is manifested in a spectacular festival.

Omak Stampede
USA

696 ● USA. A calf is immobilized with a halter during the Omak Stampede.

696-697 ● USA. A cowboy throws the lasso.

Rodeo
USA

698 ● USA. A competitor in the Cowtown Rodeo, held in New Jersey, throws himself on a bull to wrestle it to the ground.

698-699 ● USA. Having roped its horns, two cowboys win control of a young bull.

USA. A participant at
the Buffalo Bill Cody
Stampede Fourth of July
Rodeo follows a bull on
horseback.

USA. The rodeo calls for great physical effort by horses and their riders.

Rodeo
Canada

Canada.
As shown by the cowboy's
face, wrestling with a
young bull demands great
physical effort.

706 and 706-707 ● USA. The rodeo is not without a violent aspect, as by the calf's desperate flight from the mounted cowboy.

708-709 ● USA. A cowboy enters the ring.

USA. A cowboy can barely control this bucking horse in a bronco saddle-riding competition, which consists of riding a saddled foal, or bronco.

USA. During a contest, two team members attempt to control a wild horse.

714 and 715 ● USA. Remaining on a wild horse is a test that requires the utmost strength.

716-717 ● Canada. Dramatic falls are an attraction for the crowd at a rodeo.

VISIT THE HISTORIC
ROCKYVIEW HOTEL
STEAKHOUSE DANCEHALL

Rodeo
Australia

Australia. Breakaways,
falls, and roll-overs are
always a wild-card threat
at rodeos.

Australia. The powerful ringers are accustomed to falling, but the same thing cannot be said of the untamed horses participating in rodeos. In fact, the horses are the ones that usually get hurt.

Rodeo de la Semana Criolla
Uruguay

Uruguay. During Creole week in Montevideo, Argentine, Brazilian and Uruguyuan *gauchos* challenge one another in various rodeos.

• Uruguay. Horses and *gauchos* offer acrobatic displays.

AUTHORS Biographies

◼ GABRIELE BOISELLE

Gabriele Boiselle, who has worked professionally for many years, is one of the world's most famous equestrian photographers and his work is regularly presented in the most important horse-racing periodicals. He has also published a number of successful books.

◼ HENRY DALLAL

Henry Dallal, who was born in Iran, is a landscape and nature photographer. His work has appeared in such publications as The Los Angeles Times, Hermes, Country Life, The Daily Telegraph, Household Cavalry Journal and Climbing. His books include *Pageantry and Performance: The Household Cavalry in a Celebration of Pictures*, the outcome of six years of work dedicated to following the Household Cavalry of Britain's Royal Guard. The results of this project have been exhibited at Windsor Castle, Kensington Palace, and the Royal Geographical Society. Dallal was also appointed to photograph H.R.H Queen Elizabeth for the cover of *All the Queen's Horses*, a tribute to Her Majesty's Jubilee. He has also contributed to *Horse Gunners: A Photographic Record of The King's Troop of the Royal Horse Artillery*.

◼ ATTILA KORBELY

Attila Korbely, a 32-year-old nature photographer, has been taking pictures since his childhood. He has worked for the most important photo magazines, and published extensively on photography and ecology, becoming the most published nature photographer in Hungary. He has served as an equipment tester for Canon, as chief nature photographer for Hungary's National Geographic Magazine, and is currently president of Nimrod: The Hungarian Nature Photographers Society. Mr. Korbely has undertaken more than 10 photo expeditions in search of stories on musk oxen, deer, etc., and on the world's most endangered areas. He has spent many weeks from season to season with the Takhi horses on the Hungarian *puszta* and in the Pentezug Bioreservation, recording them from birth to death – playing, fighting, feeding, and breeding.

PAOLO MANILI

Paolo Manili was born in Milan in 1949. A professional journalist, horse expert and a member of the International Alliance of Equestrian Journalists, he was for many years an editor with Cavallo Magazine and Lo Sperone, and continues to contribute to these specialized monthlies. For ten years he wrote the equestrian and riding column for several leading Italian dailies (Il Resto del Carlino, La Nazione and Il Giorno). From 1976 to the present he has reported on the world's major equestrian events. Manili has also headed the press office for international show jumping events, including several World Cup qualifiers in Bologna and also the Milan Masters. He has collaborated with periodicals such as Capital, Gente Viaggi and Polo International. For years he handled the series of manuals for Edizioni Equestri, including Guida del Cavaliere. He also wrote the book *Graziano Mancinelli – La leggenda di un cavaliere* (Poligrafici Editoriale).

SENIO SENSI

Senio Sensi was born in Siena in 1941. As a journalist, he has collaborated with periodicals and television stations in Siena and outside the city. For eight years he was Governor of the Noble Contrada of the Goose and is currently Managing Director of the Consortium for the Protection of the Palio, in charge of Communications and Image for the Siena festival. He is cofounder and director of the magazine Il Carroccio di Siena, which discusses the city's history, culture and events.

MEDFORD TAYLOR

Medford Taylor was born in Conway, North Carolina. His passion for horses has been the hallmark of his thirty-year career. As a freelance photographer, he has worked for numerous international periodicals, including GEO, Newsweek, TIME and National Geographic Magazine. Taylor has won a number of prizes, notably awards from the Virginia News Photographers Association and the White House News Photographers Association, and he participated in international photo exhibitions, including the 1997 Visa Pour L'Image international photo festival in Perpignan, France.

INDEX

PHOTO CREDITS

Page 1 Gabriele Boiselle/Archiv Boiselle

Pages 2-3 Alamy images

Pages 4-5 David Stoecklein/Corbis/ Contrasto

Pages 6-7 Giampiero Sposito/Reuters/ Contrasto

Page 9 Tim Davis/Corbis/Contrasto

Page 11 Gabriele Boiselle/Archiv Boiselle

Pages 12-13 Mark Barrett

Pages 14-15 Gabriele Boiselle/Archiv Boiselle

Pages 16-17 Gabriele Boiselle/Archiv Boiselle

Page 19 Gabriele Boiselle/Archiv Boiselle

Page 23 Mark Barrett

Pages 24-25 Henry Dallal

Pages 26-27 Manfred Horvath/ Anzenberger/Contrasto

Pages 28-29 Royalty-Free/Corbis/ Contrasto

Page 31 Gabriele Boiselle/Archiv Boiselle

Page 33 Gabriele Boiselle/Archiv Boiselle

Page 39 Gabriele Boiselle/Archiv Boiselle

Pages 40-41 Gabriele Boiselle/Archiv Boiselle

Page 42 Mark Barrett

Page 43 Mark Barrett

Page 44 Mark Barrett

Page 45 Mark Barrett

Pages 46-47 Mark Barrett

Page 48 Gabriele Boiselle/Archiv Boiselle

Page 49 Gabriele Boiselle/Archiv Boiselle

Page 50 Mark Barrett

Page 51 Mark Barrett

Page 52 Mark Barrett

Page 53 Mark Barrett

Page 54 Mark Barrett

Page 55 Gabriele Boiselle/Archiv Boiselle

Page 56 Gabriele Boiselle/Archiv Boiselle

Page 57 Gabriele Boiselle/Archiv Boiselle

Pages 58-59 Mark Barrett

Page 60 Gabriele Boiselle/Archiv Boiselle

Page 61 Gabriele Boiselle/Archiv Boiselle

Pages 62-63 Gabriele Boiselle/Archiv Boiselle

Pages 64-65 Galen Rowell/Corbis/Contrasto

Page 66 Gabriele Boiselle/Archiv Boiselle

Pages 66-67 Gabriele Boiselle/Archiv Boiselle

Page 68 Alamy Images

Pages 68-69 Alamy Images

Page 70 Marielle Andresson/Archiv Boiselle

Page 71 Marielle Andresson/Archiv Boiselle

Page 72 John Cancalosi/Ardea

Page 73 Alamy images

Pages 74-75 Giovanni Simeone/Sime/Sie

Pages 76-77 Gabriele Boiselle/Archiv Boiselle

Page 77 Gabriele Boiselle/Archiv Boiselle

Pages 78-79 Gabriele Boiselle/Archiv Boiselle

Pages 80-81 Gabriele Boiselle/Archiv Boiselle

Pages 82-83 Gabriele Boiselle/Archiv Boiselle

Pages 84-85 Gabriele Boiselle/Archiv Boiselle

Pages 86-87 Gabriele Boiselle/Archiv Boiselle

Page 88 Mark Barrett

Page 89 Mark Barrett

Page 90 Mark Barrett

Page 91 Mark Barrett

Pages 92-93 Mark Barrett

Page 93 Mark Barrett

Pages 94-95 Mark Barrett

Pages 96-97 L. Lenz/Bickwinkel

Pages 98-99 Gabriele Boiselle/Archiv Boiselle

Page 100 Gabriele Boiselle/Archiv Boiselle

Page 101 Gabriele Boiselle/Archiv Boiselle

Pages 102-103 Gabriele Boiselle/Archiv Boiselle

Pages 104-105 Gabriele Boiselle/Archiv Boiselle

Page 105 Gabriele Boiselle/ Archiv Boiselle

Pages 106-107 Gabriele Boiselle/Archiv Boiselle

Page 108 Mark Barrett

Page 109 Mark Barrett

Page 110 Mark Barrett

Page 111 Mark Barrett

Page 112 Mark Barrett

Page 113 Mark Barrett

Page 114 Gabriele Boiselle/Archiv Boiselle

Page 115 Gabriele Boiselle/Archiv Boiselle

Page 116 Gabriele Boiselle/Archiv Boiselle

Page 117 Gabriele Boiselle/Archiv Boiselle

Pages 118-119 Mark Barrett

Page 120 Mark Barrett

Page 121 Mark Barrett

Page 122 left and right Mark Barrett

Page 123 Mark Barrett

Pages 124-125 Gabriele Boiselle/Archiv Boiselle

Page 126 Marielle Andresson/Archiv Boiselle

Page 127 Marielle Andresson /Archiv Boiselle

Page 128 Mark Barrett

Page 129 Mark Barrett

Pages 130-131 Mark Barrett

Pages 132-133 Mark Barrett

Page 133 Mark Barrett

Page 134 Mark Barrett

Page 135 Mark Barrett

Page 137 Gabriele Boiselle/Archiv Boiselle

Page 141 Vincent Munier/Nature Picture Library

PHOTO CREDITS

PHOTO CREDITS

● France. Big eyes, graceful features and a prominent forehead are distinctive of the magnificent Arabian horse.